Handling Usually Confused Expressions In English Language

A.P. Sharma

UNICORN

Publisher

UNICORN BOOKS

F-2/16, Ansari Road, Daryaganj, New Delhi-110002
☎ 011-23275434, 23262683, 23250704 • *Fax:* 011-23257790
E-mail: info@unicornbooks.in • *Website:* www.unicornbooks.in

Branch : Mumbai

23-25, Zaoba Wadi, Thakurdwar, Mumbai-401002
☎ 022-22010941, 022-22053387
E-mail: rapidex@bom5.vsnl.net.in

Showroom :

★ **PM Publications,** New Delhi

- 10-B, Netaji Subhash Marg, Daryaganj
  New Delhi-110002
- 6686, Khari Baoli, Delhi-110006

ISBN 978-81-7806-148-1

Handling Usually Confused Expressions in English Language

Edition: 2014

Printed at : Unique Color Carton, Maya Puri, New Delhi-110064

Dedicated to

My late wife, Mrs. Vimla Sharma,

who always inspired me to

follow the righteous path in life.

Contents

Preface

Students often get confused while writing or speaking certain words that have either almost identical spellings or pronunciation. How to mitigate such kind of confusion is a real enigma. Teachers employ different means and ways to help their students so that they may improve their English in various respects. Some teachers of composition hold that whenever a student makes mistakes, it must be identified by a red ink mark so that he/she should be discouraged to repeat that mistake. But most students don't like such sort of marking as they don't appreciate their papers to be ridden with the red ink. I remember from my own experience, while I was teaching in Africa in a Teachers' College around thirty years back, that some students really didn't like their assignments to be marked frequently with red ink even if they committed mistakes in writing. Instead they appreciated to be called privately and advised about their mistakes.

Red ink markings, however made with great care and attention on the part of the teacher, cannot possibly help students to improve their mistakes completely unless they develop good reading habits. Unfortunately, a very small number of students read or write sufficiently these days because they devote much of their valuable time in reading or writing e-mails. As a consequence, they continue with their weakness in English even if they pass a certain standard or attain degrees.

They really don't know the value of learning English correctly in schools, as they are unaware of the fact that good knowledge of spoken and written English is a basic requirement in life. When they go for business interviews or to seek jobs at a fairly respectable workplace after completing their education, they need to possess good knowledge of both, written and spoken English. Many business concerns and companies today consider Standard English as a prerequisite to offering a position in their workplaces. As such, a proper knowledge of English usage is a great requirement for all those who are desirous to be successful in life and to seek jobs or assignments at certain workplaces where English is considered as the most important medium of communication. It is, therefore, imperative to learn its usage correctly.

The truth is that our language is judged all the time by our friends, employers and teachers as well. Therefore, we need to work hard and pay good attention to improve our language by constantly practising it and repeatedly taking care of all those areas where we are weak. But is there any best way to do so? At this occasion I am reminded of a beautiful precept probably uttered inadvertently by one of the characters in the great novel titled, *The Bridge on the River Kwai*. The chief instructor at the end of the training finally instructs the three British agents who are oriented to blow off the bridge made by the Japanese at the river Kwai to enter into India straight through Burma. He says, "Remember one thing that there is always *a final action after the final action*." That is the only way to help you to improve your English if you really want to do it. It has helped me a lot in my life at several occasions after I understood its meaning correctly. Before turning in any of my assignments in the class or when I appeared at a university examination, I always revised my work many times until I was certain that

I would accomplish it very well. Perhaps it is also the secret of learning anything — learning English as well. It is therefore only through constant practice and by sufficiently revising the areas where you feel you are weak, that you can improve your own English too. There are no shortcuts to it. Just take it as a basic fact.

Paul Brians in his *Common Errors in English Usage* states, "Errors in usage are a lot like errors in table manners. There are tiny deviations from standard practice few people will notice or care about." He explains it with the help of a beautiful analogy. He says, "Using a wrong phrase in place of a right one would be like using a salad fork to eat a steak or using a term like 'decimate' to mean 'destroy'." Paul feels that a misuse or a wrong use of an English phrase would be equivalent to falling face-first into the mashed potatoes when the user really does not mean it. I present another example to highlight the issue. Two words such as 'already' and 'all ready', which have almost quite identical spellings and also pronunciation, are often misused while one uses them in sentences. 'Already' simply means before and 'all ready' means completely prepared. As soon as I complete my assignment I will be all ready. You may use the term 'already' in a sentence like, I have already completed my assignment. Thus, using a correct usage simply means to be precise and accurate in your expression without creating any confusion in the minds of the listeners. It also presents a wholesome picture of the speaker's personality before the listeners who immediately start reckoning the person from the language he/she uses before them.

Well, guidelines for usage given in this work need not to be followed with a feeling of being dragged away forcibly into a particular direction. If you like you may choose your own way and keep continuing your own style, but as far as possible you should use only a correct word or right phrase when it is required at a particular place or situation so that you are not misunderstood or underrated by others. I have tried to present a great number of usages in this book that are not quite dialectical. At the same time I have included many usages that are commonly misused even by educated people and many times such usages may be offensive to a certain kind of people or community. I have also included many phrases and words that look so simple but at times their pronunciation is different and their meanings differ tremendously when we add adjectives or prepositions to them. I have primarily chosen standard United Kingdom usage, which is largely followed in India, Australia, Canada, Nigeria, Pakistan and many other countries of the world. Only those words and usages, which create confusion as far as their meanings, spellings and pronunciations are concerned, have been included in the book. I have not taken every usage or word that apparently doesn't lead to any turmoil. Examples, providing applications of the usages and words, are provided by using appropriate sentences shown within single inverted commas.

While compiling this book, I have discussed matters relating to English usage with my old colleagues, learned people in the field including certain eminent teachers of English who have wide experience in teaching English in schools and colleges, who have kindly added to my knowledge. I believe it will also enrich the students at senior secondary, under-graduate and graduate levels, as well as help all other readers in many more ways and improve their language.

— A.P. Sharma

March 3, 2008

Camas, Washington State, USA

Widespread Errors in Handling English Language

A

abandon

The simple meaning of the term 'abandon', is 'to forsake'. For example, the cruel teacher punished the boy so hard that he was unable to move for a few minutes. 'Then he abandoned him without taking him to the hospital'.

abject

Abject is primarily used to denote 'hopeless' or 'miserable'. One cannot enjoy 'abject pleasure' unless one is trying to use it in a negative sense or to show one's critical mood.

about

If 'about' is used in an ordinary conversation, it has an abstract meaning. For example, when you have narrated everything about someone, you may say, 'It is all about him', which means you have said everything related to the particular person.

absorbtion/absorption

The right spelling of the term is 'absorption' which is a noun, but when it is used as a 'verb', it is 'absorbed' or 'absorbing'. However, absorbtion is not a correct word.

accent marks

'Accent marks' in a loose sense may mean 'to indicate all diacritical marks' helpful in understanding pronunciation correctly. Words taken from foreign languages often carry their accent marks with them. French and Italian words carry *grave* or left-leaning accent marks. In Italian, café will be written as *caffe*. It is advisable not to substitute one kind of accent mark for another.

accept/except

I will rather be happy to 'accept' soup right now than anything else. 'When I am late for dinner, I don't accept anything else except soup.'

access

The term 'access' which is a noun, can also be used as a verb sometimes. For example, you can 'access' the honourable minister even late in the night. It simply means you can reach or get access to the minister's place late in the night when normally other people are not permitted to reach him at that hour.

accessory

It means some kind of 'accomplice' or 'assistant' or 'ornament' or something like 'a handbag'. It is often mispronounced having two 'SS' in it, but it should be pronounced as 'ack' such as (ack ses' ery).

accidently/accidentally

The correct term is 'accidentally' not 'accidently'. Accidentally means 'by chance' or 'unintentionally'. 'I reached your place accidentally when I was looking for Kapoor's house.'

according to/per

'Per' and 'according to' carry the same meaning except that 'per' is used in situations like, 'As per orders of the captain she was taken away from the ship.'

acronyms and apostrophes

Recently the apostrophe is also used in plural 'acronyms' (a word formed from the initial letters of other words, such as YMCA), which is against the tradition. Some people don't accept it as correct. But it is widely observed that the use of apostrophes with terms like 'Gain knowledge of ABC's', is now commonly accepted.

acrosst/across

Acrosst is a usual misspelling of the word 'across'. It simply means 'crossways' or 'from corner to corner'. However, it has some other uses too. For example, 'When you pass the second light from here you will come across (reach) a big white building. There lives your sister.'

actual fact/actually

'Actually' is the right way and to add 'fact' to it is meaningless. 'She actually visited me last Sunday.'

adapt/adopt

The simple meaning of 'adapt' is 'to modify and accept something wilfully'. 'As they had no children, they adopted a boy from an orphanage and adapted to many of his living and eating ways to make him feel at home.'

add/ad

The term 'ad' is the short form of 'advertisement' but 'add' means 'to append' or 'to include'. 'I gave an ad in a local newspaper but when I sent the same ad to a national newspaper I added one more sentence to it.'

adieu/ado

'Adieu' means 'goodbye'; and 'ado' means 'fuss' or 'trouble'. 'Finally I bade her adieu last night when she was leaving the town for good.' 'Without further ado, the child did as instructed.'

administer/minister

The simple meaning of 'administer' is to 'manage', 'direct' or 'govern'. The magistrate 'administered' the oath to the minister. We need to add 'to' after the term 'minister' when we use it as a verb. 'While ministering to her the right medicine, she administered the tools carefully.'

adultry/adultery

'Adultery' is the correct spelling, and it is incorrect to use 'adultry' for it. The term 'adultery' is used to refer to illicit relationship when out of the two, one partner is cheating on his spouse.

advance/advanced

'Advance' is used to denote that someone has the information or the secret before it was actually known to others. 'I learnt it in advance that he would be at home by 9 PM last night.' 'The allied forces advanced (moved forward) against the enemy in spite of heavy shelling against them.'

adverse/averse

I went through 'adverse' (difficult or unpleasant) circumstances when I was graduating from the University. My friend Satish was often 'averse' (disliked or disinclined) to me when I was on the road to progress.

advice/advise

The term 'advice' is a noun and 'advise' is a verb. 'I advised her to keep away from him and take this advice for good.' Quite often people don't use these terms correctly.

affect/effect

The word 'affect' is used as a verb and 'effect' as a noun except that at times (very rarely) some people use 'effect' as a verb too. 'The effect of your medicine affected me so well that I recovered soon.' 'When she showed her anger towards me she meant to effect (influence or create) the entire environment of the house.'

affluence/effluence

The simple meaning of the term 'affluence' is 'riches'. 'Effluence' means 'toxic waste or litter'. 'When someone has wealth he/she is affluent; wealth brings affluence.' 'All this dirt lying by the roadside is total effluence.'

agree/agree with

The word 'agree' may look a simple term but it has several meanings when used in different situations. Its simple meaning is 'consent' or 'yes'. 'As I implored her earnestly, she agreed to go with me at once.' The meaning of 'agree with' is 'be of the same opinion' or 'be in harmony with'. 'Her letter does not agree with what she had said earlier.'

agreeance/agreement

'Agreeance' is often confused with 'agreement' which means 'in harmony with' or 'in accord with'. 'When one agrees with you one is in agreement.'

ain't/am not/aren't

'Ain't' was used in the past in place of 'isn't' or 'aren't'. It was originally meant to be used for 'am not'. Except using it casually when you intend to cajole someone, its use is improper these days.

all/all of

The simple meaning of 'all' is 'whole number of'. 'All' horses are animals but not 'all' animals are horses. 'All' also suggests at times 'what one values most'. She lost her 'all' when she was a child. The phrase 'all of' has a varied meaning that many people may not really conceive. It means 'everything' or 'everyone'. 'All of them wanted to go to the railway station.'

all goes well/augurs well

When someone asks you, 'How are things with you these days?', you may simply reply him/her, 'All goes well.' But to confuse 'augurs well', which means extending information 'based on omens', will be an erroneous use of the term in this context.

all of the sudden/all of a sudden

Something happening unexpectedly could be indicated by 'all of a sudden'. She got her new job 'all of a sudden'. 'All of the sudden' is an incorrect use for 'all of a sudden'.

all ready/already

The phrase 'all ready' means 'completely ready'. 'When you arrived at my place I was all ready to receive you.' 'Already' means something that has happened before a particular time. 'When they reached my place, I had already gone.'

all right/alright

The correct phrase is 'all right' which means 'yes' or 'okay' or 'no problem'. It is only sometimes that people or the press may use 'alright' too.

all the farther/as far as

Some people may (rarely) use 'all the farther' to denote distance in mind or on land. You cannot get them even if you go 'all the farther'. Better use would be 'You cannot get them 'as far as' you go. Or, 'As far as you go, you will find the place all green.'

all together/altogether

'All together' is a phrase that means 'in a group'. We gathered 'all together' at her house that night. 'Altogether' is an adverb that means 'completely' or 'totally'. 'She was altogether happy to see me also in her birthday party.'

alleged

It means someone who is 'suspected' of a crime. 'He is alleged to have committed the crime.' It does not mean that he/she has certainly committed the crime. The word simply indicates a 'suspected criminal' or 'a crime'.

allegory

When someone presents 'a parallel example' or 'a similar situation' the word 'allegory' is used.

alliterate/illiterate

'She is totally illiterate as she cannot read or write at all.' Alliteration means a string of words having the same initial sound, placed in succession in a sentence. For example, 'Pink pot of potatoes.'

alls/all

'All she remembers is that she has never seen him before.' The 'alls' is at times expressed to mean 'all is' which is not much in vogue these days.

allude/elude

'Allude' is used 'to refer' to something. One can 'allude' to one's son's qualities. 'Elude' means 'to escape'. 'When she was alleged to have committed that theft, she tried to elude arrest.'

allude/refer

When we use 'allude' to refer something we mean 'referring indirectly'; but when we 'refer' to something, we are not ambiguous in our 'referring to it'. Besides this difference, both the terms indicate to referring only.

allusion/illusion

A 'mirage' or a magic trick could be taken to be an 'illusion'. When one travels through a deep desert during summer, one may see water instead of sand. It is a kind of 'illusion'. An 'allusion' is a 'reference' or a 'citation' or a 'quotation' from a book or an article.

almost

The word 'almost' should precede immediately the word or phrase it modifies. 'He spent almost two hundred rupees on our dinner.'

almost always/most always

'Almost always' is the more acceptable expression than 'most always', which is a slangy way of expressing it. Besides, 'almost always' also indicates a greater frequency about some action or a thing or person. 'She is almost always there in the library when I happen to be there.'

alot/a lot

'Alot' is not a correct word to use in place of 'a lot', which simply indicates a 'great quantity of a thing or action'. 'She used to visit her sister a lot when she was in college.'

altar/alter

An 'altar' is the platform in front of a temple or a religious place like a church. When we use 'alter' we mean 'to change'. 'I wish to alter my plans for visiting Goa next month.'

alternate/alternative

Sometimes some people use 'alternate' for alternative. The most accepted term is 'alternative', except that when you say, 'We all friends meet at the station on alternate Sundays,' you need to use the term 'alternate'.

alumnus/alumni

'Alumnus' means a singular male and 'alumna' means a singular female. To use the terms correctly one must distinguish between the singular and the plural forms. When we mean to indicate a singular person we say one alumnus, but when indicating plural, we say alumni. 'It was a great gathering of alumni at the school.'

amature/amateur

'Amature' is not the correct form in English but 'amateur' is, which means 'a part-timer' who cultivates an art for his/her personal pleasure and not as a profession. 'He is an amateur violinist who plays it for his own pleasure.'

ambiguous/ambivalent

The simple meaning of 'ambiguous' is 'unclear', 'vague' and 'indefinite'. 'Whenever he talks to me he is ambiguous and I am not able to get him.' 'Ambivalent' means 'unsure', 'undecided' and having 'two minds'. 'Many times she is ambivalent so she is indecisive about her plans.'

ambivalent/indifferent

If one is 'ambivalent' about a problem he is 'unclear or vague' about it, but if he is 'indifferent' about it, it would mean that he has 'no particular concern' about it or he is indifferent to it.

amongst/among

'Amongst' and 'among' both, mean 'amid' or 'in the midst of'. But the term commonly used is 'among' not 'amongst'.

amoral/immoral

The simple meaning of 'amoral' is 'unrelated to morality'. Its extended meaning could be taken as 'unprincipled'. But 'immoral' means 'unethical'. 'Some people are totally immoral in their conduct because their way of thinking might be amoral.'

amount/number

The term 'amount' is related to the 'quantity of things'. When we use 'number', we mean we could 'count' the things.

amuse/bemuse

She 'bemused' us by her tricks. It means that more than entertainment she 'confused' the people. The term 'amuse' simply means to 'entertain'. 'She amused us all by her tricks.'

analog/analogy/analogue

'Analogy' means 'similarity' or 'likeness' or 'parallel'. 'Analogue' implies 'something having analogy to something else'. 'Different human hearts are analogous as far as their shapes are concerned but in size they are not the same.' 'Analog' is an American term for the British term 'analogue'.

and also/and, also

'And also' is out of use or redundant. It is better to use either 'and' or 'also'. 'She came to see her father and her husband also came along with her.'

anecdote/antidote

These two words though look quite akin but they are very different in meaning and use. 'Anecdote' means 'small tales that are amusing and entertaining'. 'He amuses us constantly by his anecdotes.' 'When someone takes a wrong medicine and gets sick, the doctor prescribes antidotes to cure him.'

angel/angle

An 'angel' is a 'heaven related entity' but a triangle has three 'angles'. People often get confused in spelling these two terms.

anticlimatic/anticlimactic

The term anticlimatic is incorrect. 'Anticlimactic' conveys the sense when during a discourse 'one descends from a height to a lower level of talks'. It is related with 'climaxes' and not to 'climate'. Often people get confused about the two terms.

anti-social/asocial

'Asocial' simply means a person who is less social with the people, but 'anti-social' is a person who acts against the interests of a society. One, who is a thief or a dacoit or a murderer, is an 'anti-social' person.

anxious/eager

The term 'anxious' implies 'worrying' more than being 'desirous' for something. But 'eager' purely indicates 'worry-free wantingness' or 'desire'. 'I am eager to see my cousin whom I haven't seen for years.' 'I am anxious about my son who has started living in a hostel now.'

anymore/any more

The common spelling of the phrase is 'any more' and it is mostly used in the middle or end (not in the beginning) of a negative expression. A bookstall may exhibit: 'We don't keep books on Geography any more.' One can also use it while questioning. 'Do you have any more books on the subject of romance?'

anytime/any time

Traditionally it is a two-word term misused at times as one word. 'You can visit me any time you like to.'

anyways/anyway

Both, 'anyways' and 'anyway' can sometimes be used in the beginning of a sentence by a speaker when he/she starts narrating or concluding matters. 'Anyways, I ended my entire talk in this manner and tried hard to convince them about the disputed issue.' These expressions are not a part of formal English. A more common use of the term in formal English is a two-word phrase 'any way'. 'Any way, can you convince her that I need her earnestly?'

apart/a part

The term 'apart' implies separation but the two-word phrase indicates 'togetherness' or 'union'. 'Both the persons fell apart after living together as close friends for fifteen years.' 'My wife is a part of my life.'

apex/climax

'Apex' means top or highest point. 'This is the apex of this building.' 'Climax' means the most exciting or important event or point in time. 'The election campaign is at its climax these days.'

appraise/apprise

When one guesses the value of a thing, one 'appraises', but when one informs others about a situation, one 'apprises' about it. 'The broker appraised the new buyer about a possible value of the house he wanted to buy.' 'He also apprised the buyer about the merits and demerits of the newly built house.'

apropos/appropriate

The term 'apropos' is used to denote 'relevance' in connection with what has already been said or narrated. In that sense it falls quite near to the term 'appropriate' in meaning though it does not convey exactly the same meaning. 'Your explanations about the night clubs were apropos to what had already been said about them.' The meaning of 'appropriate' is 'suitable' or 'apt' or 'fitting'. 'The story you narrated was appropriate in view of the prevailing circumstances in their family.' 'The girl, you found for his son for marriage, is quite an appropriate match for him.'

approve/approve of

The word 'approve' means 'endorse' or 'back up'. 'I approve your suggestions.' 'Approve of' means to 'give one's approval'. It also means 'to confirm' or 'to agree to'. 'Your father will always approve of your marriage with the girl you have in mind.'

aspect/expect

'Aspect' implies 'a particular part or feature of something'. 'Please examine every aspect of this plan before launching it.' 'Expect' means 'to look forward to something'. 'I was expecting your call tomorrow.'

artic/arctic

'Arctic' is the correct word originating from the term Arctic Circle. 'Artic' is not accepted usually.

artical/article

Only 'article' (a piece of writing) is the correct spelling, not 'artical'. 'Your article on "Human Rights", appeared in *The Times of India* yesterday, was really highly informative.'

as/as

The adverb 'as' has several uses in spoken and written English. When another 'as' is used in a sentence, it shows a kind of comparison of the same degree. 'She is as tall as her senior sister.' 'As' is also used to indicate the adverbs '*when*' or '*while*'. 'I saw him as he was entering the theatre.' It is also used to indicate '*since*'. 'As she was late she could not accompany us.'

as follow/as follows

The correct form is 'as follows' and not 'as follow'. 'My instructions are as follows.'

as if/like

It is always good to use 'as if' when we are involved in formal writing. For example, 'The boy sitting at the bank of the river looks so eager as if he would jump into it soon.' 'Like' is used informally in normal conversation. 'He took to music like a professional from the very beginning.'

as of yet/yet

The term 'as of yet' is not a common or a correct use in English and it does not certainly replace 'yet'. 'Yet' has a better and appropriate use. For example, 'Though she worked very hard, yet the percentage of marks she got at the final examination was not so high.'

as per/in accordance with

It looks that both these terms are quite redundant now and are not in use, except that some people may use it without knowing that such a use is often meaningless. 'In accordance with' (as per) your desire we are submitting the items you thought necessary to be submitted for further action.' In its place, it looks better to write, 'As you desired, we are submitting the items for further action.'

assure/ensure/insure

When we 'assure' someone of something, we make him/her confident that it would be done. It is a kind of promise that will be fulfilled under any kind of odds. 'I assure you of my help whatever difficulties may come in the way.' When we use the term 'insure' we mean to issue an insurance policy. 'You can be insured for Rupees Two Lakhs even though you have reached that age.' However, the term 'ensure' simply means 'to make sure' or 'to make certain'. 'You should ensure that she will reach the station on time.'

asterick/asterisk

'Asterick' is a wrong spelling of the term 'asterisk' (*) which is indicated after a word or a sentence by a little star to highlight it. Often people spell it incorrectly and also pronounce it erroneously.

augur/auger

The term 'augur' is a verb that means 'foretell'. 'He often augurs quite correctly.' 'Auger' is a wrong spelling of the word 'augur'.

aural/oral

'Aural' is related with the 'things we hear', and 'oral' with the things that 'we say or speak'. 'It is an aural device which is used when you like to listen to music.' 'Your pronunciation is mostly judged by your oral speech.'

awhile/a while

Both the terms imply quite akin meanings except their use is different in written English. 'Awhile' simply means 'for sometime' or 'for a time'. 'Could you permit me to work at your place awhile?' But when it comes after the preposition *for*, we normally separate 'a' from while. 'Could you permit me to work at your place for a while?'

axel/axle

An 'axle' is the 'centre of a wheel. 'I fear that the axle of the front right wheel of my car is slightly bent.' 'Axel', which means a jump in figure skating, has been termed after the name of Axel Paulson.

B

babble out

The term 'babble' means 'talk nonsense'. 'She often babbles out in such a way, that we cannot comprehend her.' It also means to 'make a sound like a baby'. 'You often babble, so nothing is clear to us.'

back

The simple meaning of 'back' is to go backwards. 'Can you go two steps back to accommodate her also?'

back up/back down/back out

'Back up' means 'support'. 'A good friend always backs up in rainy days.' 'Back down' means to 'give up a claim'. 'She has backed down from the position she took last Sunday.' 'Back out' implies 'withdrawal from a promise' or 'withdrawal from an understanding'. 'Some people easily back out from their promise when they are most needed.' However, there are some other uses of the term 'back' when it is suffixed with a few words. For example, 'back bone' would mean 'a strong or a sure support'. 'He is always my back bone.'

backward/backwards

Both the words are good in English but more common in use is 'backward'. As an adjective, simply 'backward' will be good and be acceptable. 'Many of the Indian villages are still backward with no electricity.' As an adverb, we can use either of these two words. 'Please put my shirt backward (towards the rear).'

bad/badly

Use of 'bad' as an adjective is easier in a sentence than 'badly' which is an adverb. For example, 'When I saw him I felt 'bad' as he looked very miserable.' It would be wrong to say, 'I felt badly.' But 'badly' can be used in situations like, 'She required your help badly when you were away from the town.'

barb wire/barbed wire

Most common use is 'barbed wire' and not 'barb wire'. We often put 'barbed wire' around an outfield to protect it from animals.

bare/bear

The simple meaning of the term 'bare' is 'nude' or 'exposed' or 'uncovered'. 'When I saw him he was bare-footed.' 'Bear' means an animal having massive body with coarse heavy fur and with relatively short limbs. It also means 'to contain' or 'to reflect'. 'This document bears your signatures.' 'This shirt bears the name of the company that made it.'

bear oneself/bear against

'Bear oneself' implies 'presenting oneself in a special way'. 'He bears himself like a great actor.' 'Bear against' means 'to possess in the heart or mind'. 'She bears a grudge against me for no reason.'

based around/ based on

'Based on' is the traditional expression that means 'rooted in' or 'derived from'. 'My belief is based on what I heard from my mother's mouth when I was young.' 'Based around' is not commonly acceptable for the term based on.

basicaly/basically

'Basically' is the right expression and 'basicaly' is a misuse of the term basically (adverb), which means 'essentially' or principally. 'I basically stand in your support when you contest the next elections.'

bazaar/bizarre

The simple meaning of 'bazaar' is 'market'. This term is also commonly used in Hindi language in which it also means a 'market'. 'Bizarre' means 'strange' or 'peculiar'. 'His appearance on the stage was quite bizarre from the point of view of his dress and gait.'

because/due to/since

These three terms carry almost similar meanings, which convey the sense of 'owing to' or 'by reason of', but they are used in different situations in different sentences conveying the same meaning. For example, 'I could not come to your place because I had not finished my home work.' 'Since I did not finish my home work I did not come to see you.' 'I did not come to your place due to my home work that I could not complete on time.' It depends on the speaker how to use them in a sentence, but their meaning does not change to any extent.

behaviours/behaviour

'Behaviour' is the right term to be used except that psychologists or anthropologists or sociologists may use it as 'behaviours' in plural form in their writings. 'Behaviour' simply means 'conduct' or 'a pattern of action'. 'You were quite submissive in your behaviour (behavior is American spelling) before the elders.'

beside/besides

The term 'beside' implies 'next to'. 'She was sitting beside me in the theatre.' 'Besides' means 'in addition to'. 'Besides Romesh, two other friends also joined the picnic on the last Sunday.'

better

The word 'better' has several uses in English that the reader needs to be acquainted with. Its simple meaning is 'of superior quality' or of 'superior value, use, desirability, or acceptability'. 'It is better to reach the station before time.' 'Better you should accompany him on the tour.' 'She should better leave the place at once', which means that it will be good for her to leave the place at once for certain reasons contained in the mind of the speaker.

bias/biased

The word 'bias' is a noun, which means 'prejudice' or 'unfairness' or 'a preconceived notion'. 'Biased' is a verb. 'Since she possessed a bias against me, she was always biased towards me.' One can also be positively biased towards someone. 'He was so biased towards his son that he always pleaded for him.' 'Biased' is also used as an adjective. 'It was a completely biased report.'

bid for/bid up/bid on

The meaning of 'bid' is 'proposal' or 'offer'. It has so many connotations when suffixed with prepositions like for, up, and on, etc. The meaning of 'bid for' is to 'make an offer of money'. 'I would like to bid for this car.' 'Bid up' means 'to make a higher offer'. 'The house was bid up far beyond its real value.' The meaning of 'bid on' is 'to put in a tender for'. 'The manager decided to bid on the old car.'

blatant

Th · meaning of 'blatant' is 'offensively noisy'. But the term can be applied to any kind of unworthy conduct. 'He became suddenly blatant in his behaviour at the temple.'

board/above board/across the board

The word 'board' means 'a plank' (noun) and 'get on' or 'go on board' (verb). 'She boarded the plane last night.' But its meaning differs when we prefix or suffix a preposition to it. The term 'above board' means 'without any deception'. It may also refer to someone's 'honest conduct'. 'Our Prime Minister is above board in all respects.' 'Across the board' means 'far-reaching' 'all-embracing' or 'universal'. 'The factory workers' wages were raised across the board.'

boatload/buttload

The correct expression is 'boatload', which means 'a lot'. 'She got a boatload praises for her kind behaviour.' 'Buttload' is not a correct expression.

bonafied/bona fide

'Bonafied' is a wrong use of the term 'bona fide', which means 'genuine'. 'Whenever your driver's licence is checked at a store it is done to check your bona fides.'

bored of/bored with

The meaning of the phrase 'bored with' is 'tired of' or 'fed up with'. 'I am bored with your long speeches.' 'Bored of' is an incorrect usage.

born out of/born of

'Born of' implies 'cultivated' or 'developed'. 'My love for music is born of listening to Lata Mangeshkar's songs from my childhood.' The term 'born out of' is a misuse in place of the right term born of.

borrow/loan

The person requesting someone to get 'an article' or 'money' or 'anything', 'borrows' it from him/her. But the one who gives it, 'loans' it to him/her.

both/each

One has to be very careful when using 'both' or 'each' in a sentence for it could be confusing at times to use one for the other. For example, if you say, 'He gave both of us new socks.' It would mean both the persons got new socks. But if you say, 'He gave both hundred rupees', it might create confusion because it is not clear whether each one got one hundred rupees separately or both shared the money. In that case it would be better to say, 'Each one of us got hundred rupees'.

bought/brought

'Bought' is the past tense or past participle of buy. 'She bought a beautiful dress last night.' Similarly, 'brought' is the past participle of bring. 'He brought a new television two days back.'

bouyant/buoyant

'Buoyant' means 'cheerful' or 'lighthearted'. It is an accepted spelling but not 'bouyant'. 'He is often looked buoyant in his outlook and demeanor.'

bran new/brand new

The correct term is 'brand new' and not 'bran new', which sometimes some people use erroneously to indicate some special thing. 'It is a brand new cap in style and texture.' I brought it from the market yesterday.' 'Sometimes some shopkeepers keep brand new names of their shops to attract customers.'

breach/breech

The term 'breach' means 'break' or 'infringement'. 'A small breach can be seen on the upper side of this dam.' 'There was some kind of breach in their relationship.' 'Breech' means 'back part of the gun barrel where bullet is place'.

break

'Break' is just a simple word and it can be used in different situations. Its simple meaning is 'to stop'. 'Please break the speed of your car.' Break is also used to denote 'short holidays'. 'We had a break during Easter.' When someone 'gets bored or needs some space of time or desires to get relaxed', the term break can be used. 'Please give me a break. I am really tired with your problem.'

break into/break off/break out/break away

'Break into' means 'to force one's way into'. 'Some thieves broke into my apartment last night.' 'Break off' implies 'to stop temporarily'. 'Let us break off for a brief lunch now.' 'Break out' means 'a sudden appearance or start'. 'Riots in two communities broke out last night.' 'Break through' implies 'to make a way through'. 'I was able to break through the problem after an hour's hard labour.' 'Break away' means 'go away suddenly or abruptly'. 'The freedom fighters broke away the police cordon and disappeared in a few minutes in the dark.'

breath/breathe

'Breathe' is a verb and 'breath' is a noun. 'When you do yoga, you are required to tone up your breath by regulating your breathing.'

bring/take/fetch

When someone is standing away from you, you can say, 'Bring that teapot to me.' If someone is tracking or going away from you, you may say, 'Take this teapot to her if you want to have some tea.' But if someone is required to go away from you and also needs to come back to you or vice versa, you use the term 'fetch'. 'Please fetch a cup of tea for me.' It would mean to go or come after and bring or take back.

bring about/bring back/bring out/bring round

'Bring about' means 'cause to happen'. 'The Parliament has brought about many changes in the Constitution after Independence.' 'Bring back' means 'to return' or 'to cause to remember'. 'Please don't forget to bring back my medicines.' 'Bring out' implies a sense 'to appear' or 'to show clearly'. 'The newspaper will bring out the news in the morning edition.' 'Bring round' means 'to cause or regain consciousness or to yield'. 'Though we tried hard, we could not bring her round to get the required information.'

build on

'Build on' implies 'to utilise' or 'to develop' or 'to exploit'. 'One can build on one's reputation and get respect from others if one is honest and straightforward, but if he/she is not, then one is conceited.'

burn/burned

'Burn' means 'to be on fire' or 'flame' or 'glow'. 'Burned' is the past tense of the verb 'burn'. 'She was burned when she was lighting her stove.' 'She wanted to burn wood all the night.'

but/but for

'But' has several uses in English language and can be used in different situations. It implies 'only'. It is also used 'to coordinating' as a conjunction. 'We all were there in the function but (except) you.' 'I did my best to bring them close but I could not.' The term 'but for' implies 'except for', or 'without'. 'We could have not come out of that chaos but for you.'

by/buy/bye

'By' is a common preposition and can be used in sentences like, 'He must have reached home 'by' now.' In this case it indicates 'time' as well as 'possibility' of completing an action. The word 'buy' simply means to 'purchase'. 'I can buy a car by next month.' 'Bye' is a short form of 'good bye'.

by in large/by and large

The correct expression is 'by and large' which sometimes is used erroneously as 'by in large'. 'By and large' implies 'generally'. 'By and large most of the people from this country go to the church on each Sunday for prayers.'

C

cabbie/cabby

Both 'cabbie' and 'cabby' refer to 'a driver of a cab'. 'Cabbies' plural of cabby, is used commonly as slang during ordinary conversation.

callous/calloused

The term 'callous' means 'hard-hearted' or 'heartless' or 'pitiless' or 'uncaring'. 'She is a callous person.' 'Calloused' means 'coarse' or 'rough' or 'hardened'. 'He seems to be a very strong person as his hands and feet are calloused.'

call/call for/call upon

The simple meaning of 'call' is 'to name' or 'to describe' or 'to give a call' or 'to make a phone call'. 'She called (phoned) me very early this morning.' 'Call for' means 'to predict'. 'The newspapers call for early rains this year.' 'Call upon' is often used to mention someone 'visiting'. 'They intend to call upon us this afternoon.'

cavalry/Calvary

A number of soldiers mounted on horses are called a 'cavalry'. But 'Calvary' is referred to the hill on which Jesus Christ was crucified.

cannot/can not

Both the spellings are correct and mean the same, except that, if one wants to use it separately at times, it would mean putting stress on 'not'. 'I can *not* reach there on time today.'

canon/cannon

The term 'canon' means 'a principle' or 'a precept' or a 'tenet'. 'Buddha said, "Anyone who is born must die some day." It is a canon found out by Buddha.' But when we say 'cannon' we mean 'large artillery'. 'Cannons were fired from the enemy lines last night.'

capital/capitol

A 'capital' is the headquarters of a State or of a country, whereas a 'capitol' is a great building in a town. 'Delhi is the capital city of India.'

carat/caret/carrot

Most precious stones and metals are weighed in 'carats'. 'Carrots' are vegetables, which people like to eat as salads or sometimes cook them also. A 'caret' is a mark made by a proofreader on a text to indicate that at that particular place something needs to be added or to be corrected.

catalog/catalogue

Both the terms mean 'list' or 'index'. If you want to find out whether a particular item is available in this store, please check it from the 'catalogue' contained in a register. In fact, catalogue is the traditional spelling of the term and catalog is an Americanised spelling.

care

The word 'care' means 'to pay attention or to give a thought'. 'She cares a lot for all of us.'

care about/care for/care to

'Care about' implies 'to feel interest, anxiety or sorrow'. 'She failed in the examination, as she did not care about her studies at all.' 'Care for' implies to indicate 'liking' or 'to have something'. 'Do you care for a cup of tea right now?' It would mean, 'Do you want to have a cup of tea now?' 'Care to' would mean 'willingness' or 'liking'. 'I don't care to meet him right now.'

carry

'Carry' simply means 'to support the weight of and move from one place to another.' 'Please carry this book to your father.' There could be a lot of confusion when an adjective is suffixed to the term 'carry' as its meaning is changed completely.

carry away/carry far/carry back/carry forward

'Carry away' implies 'causing to lose'. 'The tide carried away the boat.' 'Carry far' implies 'make longer or extend'. 'He cannot carry far in life with the habits he possesses right now.' 'Carry back' would mean 'to keep back in the memory' or 'to recall'. 'Your tale carried them back to their childhood days.' 'Carry forward' implies 'transferring something to next page', or 'to next item', or 'to someone'. 'Could you carry forward this message to your boss?'

cast/caste

People often get confused between these two terms as their spellings are not very much different. 'Cast' means 'to throw' or 'to fling'. 'Please don't cast this dress away as it belongs to your mother.' 'Caste' means social groups different from the other groups. 'There are different kinds of castes in India based on traditions, professional practices and qualities.'

catch

The simple meaning of 'catch' is 'stopping by getting hold of something' by hands. It can be used as a noun or as a verb. 'Please catch (verb) the ball and throw that catch (noun) to me.' Like carry, 'catch' has different meanings when suffixed with prepositions.

catch on/catch up

'Catch on' implies 'to get the meaning of' or 'to understand'. 'You speak so fast that often I don't catch you on.' 'Catch up' implies 'overtaking'. 'Can she catch up with her brother in studies as she is much behind him?'

celibate/chaste

The meaning of 'celibate' is 'to remain unmarried'. One can be a 'celibate' without being 'chaste' and 'chaste' without being a 'celibate'. 'Chaste' means 'pure with respect to unlawful sexual intercourse' or 'virtuous'. 'A lawfully married woman can have sex with her husband everyday and still she is considered as a chaste person.' 'One, who is a celibate, is unmarried but it is not necessary that he has no sex with anyone.' Therefore these two terms need to be understood well.

cement/concrete

'Cement' is 'a kind of grey powder that is used to make concrete'. 'Concrete' is the 'combination of cement, water, sand and gravel.' It is used for making buildings.

centre of attraction/centre of attention

The most common phrase is 'centre of attention' and not 'centre of attraction'.

certain/certainly

The simple meaning of the term 'certain' is 'settled, of which there is no doubt'. 'It is certain that she will abide by her promise.' 'Certainly', which is an adverb, also implies the 'sense of definiteness' or 'surety'. 'If you certainly need his help, just approach him now.'

champ at the bit/chomp at the bit

'Champ at the bit' is a commonly accepted usage (not, chomp at the bit) meaning 'gnash' or 'clench' or 'grind'. Since it is not a familiar usage, people often make mistake to use it correctly.

change

'Change' means 'leave one place and go to another place' or 'to take off' or 'to put on'. 'Please change your shirt as it is dirty now.'

change to/change for/change from

'Change to' is used to 'alter the position'. For example, 'Will you please like to change to a higher gear as your car is not pulling on well?' 'Change for' implies 'to change a dress'. 'I like to change for the dinner.' It would mean that I like to change my dress for the dinner. 'Change over' implies 'changing over from one custom or tradition to another'. 'I have changed over from left-hand driving to the right-hand driving.'

Check

'Check' means 'examining something to know whether it is correct'. 'Please check this account and make the payment.' Though 'check' is a simple term, it has several meanings in English language and many more when some prepositions are suffixed to it.

check in/check out/check upon

'Check in' means to register in a hotel at the arrival. 'I shall check in the hotel around 12 noon today.' Similarly, 'check out' implies 'leaving a hotel after clearing the accounts'. 'He checked out the hotel after 1 PM today.' 'Check upon' implies 'having control'. 'Please keep a check upon the activities of your workers in the factory.'

chick/chic

'Chic' is a French originated term which means 'stylish' or 'fashionable'. 'Chick' means 'a baby bird' or 'a chicken'.

chunk/chuck

The term 'chuck' is a casual and informal term, meaning 'throw' or 'hurl'. 'Please chuck (drop) me out at the post office.' Some people may use erroneously 'chunk' instead of chuck. It is not only incorrect but also has a different meaning than 'chuck'. It means 'a large piece' or 'lump' etc.

church/Church

When 'Church' is capitalised, it refers to Roman Catholic Church. Otherwise normally when people talk about church, it is not capitalised.

cite/site/sight

These three terms are quite confusing as far as their pronunciation and meanings are concerned. 'One cites (quotes) from a book. One goes for sight-seeing after visiting the site on a Web.'

clean

'Clean' means 'free from dirt'. 'Better clean your room today.' It also implies 'purity', 'innocence' and 'no wrongdoings'. 'Swami Vivekananda had a clean life.'

clean out/clean up

'Clean out' implies 'winning' or 'taking all the money'. 'She cleaned him out by her dirty tricks.' 'Clean up' means 'to put in order'. 'We cleaned up the accounts after four hours of hard work.'

clear

The meaning of the term 'clear' implies 'free from obstruction' or 'easily seen'. 'It is a clear picture of his conduct.'

clear about/clear of/clear from/clear out

'Clear about' implies 'free from doubt or difficulty'. It also means 'certainty'. I am absolutely 'clear about' your plans. 'Clear of' means 'free from suspicion'. 'She told the client, "You are clear of all the charges now."' 'Clear from' implies 'to remove' or 'to get rid of what is not required'. 'Please clear you from any sort of doubts in this case.' 'Clear out' conveys the sense of 'going away' or 'leaving'. 'Better you clear out of her way if you wish to live peacefully.'

cleanup/clean up

The term 'cleanup' is normally used as a noun. 'The cleanup of this awfully dirty site would cost us a lot before we build a market on it.' 'Clean' is a verb and can be used in different situations in a sentence. 'As some guests are likely to visit us tomorrow, clean up the living room first.'

cliché/clichéd

'Cliché' means 'stereotyped' or 'not quite impressive'. 'The play staged last night was absolutely cliché.' The term 'cliched' can be used referring to cliché. 'Something which is cliché is clichéd.'

click/clique

'Click' is often used in place of 'clique', by mistake. 'Click' means 'a slight, sharp sound'. 'She made a small click from her mouth.' 'Clique' means 'small groups of people' to support or oppose something. 'There are many political cliques in this company.'

collaborate/corroborate

'Collaborate' means 'to share work or labour'. 'When people work together on a project they collaborate, while people who stand in testimony as a witness corroborate.' The term 'corroborate' simply means 'to confirm' or 'support'.

close

'Close' has several uses in English language. Let people not get confused to use it incorrectly. 'Close' means 'near in space or time'. 'She lives close to me.' 'Close' has another meaning too. 'Please close the doors tightly when I am gone.'

close up/close by/close down

'Close up' is used to indicate 'a close view'. 'Please take a close up of this scene.' 'Close by' means 'near'. 'He lives just close by.' 'Close down' is used to indicate 'shutting down a business'. 'The business (shop) was closed down because of poor clientele.'

coarse/course/ in due course

'Coarse' means 'crude' or 'rude' or 'rough'. This word is often misspelled as 'course', which means 'route' or 'way' or 'track' or 'curriculum'. 'In due course' means 'natural order'. 'Please don't worry for her. She will recover in due course of time.'

Columbia/Colombia

Both these words are based on Columbus, the explorer. US capital Washington D.C. (District of Columbia) is also named after him.

compare to/compare with

When one is 'stressing similarities between two or more items', one needs to use 'to' after 'compare'. 'She always likes to compare her bedroom furniture to her neighbour's bedroom furniture.' When one likes to examine both similarities and dissimilarities one should put 'with' after 'compare'. 'I don't like to compare my driving skills with that of the others.'

compliment/complement

'Compliment' is an expression denoting praise, admiration or approval. 'Whenever I wear this dress, my friends compliment me.' 'Complement' means something that contributes new or contrasting features or qualities that make it complete. 'Rice is an excellent complement to a curry dish.'

connaisseur/connoisseur

The term 'connoisseur' meaning 'expert' or 'authority' or 'specialist', is an English word, which initially has been taken from the French word '*connaisseur*'. 'He is a connoisseur as far as tasting wine is concerned.'

consensus/concensus

'Consensus' implies 'in accord' or 'in agreement' or 'in harmony' or 'to have consent'. 'Let us have everyone's consensus on this tricky issue.' Generally consensus is misspelled as concensus.

convince/persuade

Some people get confused between these two words and may take them as the same. In fact, they are quite different in meaning. Well, 'persuading' may imply 'convincing', for when one is persuaded and agrees to accept something, he/she is also likely to be convinced. But 'convincing' may involve a lot of reasoning or arguments than in 'persuading' someone. 'Persuading' involves more of an 'emotional exploitation' or 'external pressure' at times. For example, 'I was convinced after listening to her arguments and was ready to lend her money she requested.' 'She persuaded me finally to lend her some money.'

cops/corpse

A 'cop' is a police officer. 'Corpse' means a dead body. 'I saw a corpse this morning.'

copy and paste/cut and paste

'Cut and paste' is the most familiar phrase than 'copy and paste' which is not only uncommon but may be misleading as well.

copywrite/copyright/copywright

'Copyright' is the correct terminology which means securing rights on some written material. 'Copywright' or 'Copywrite' are not the correct terms to use.

continual/continuous

'Continuous' actions are 'uninterrupted' activities. 'She played chess continuously between 6 AM until 7 PM yesterday.'

A 'continual' activity may not involve continuous action. 'She tells me continually to wear a neck-tie when I go to office.'

control/control of/control over (on)

'Control' means 'power' or 'authority to direct'. 'The principal of this school has a great control on both, his staff and students.' 'Children need to be kept under the control of the principal.' 'Control over' implies 'authority' or 'management'. 'The Director of this company must have total control over his employees.'

cool/cool down (off)

Like some other words, 'cool' has also several uses in English language. 'Cool' means 'neither warm nor cold but in between'. 'Sit under this umbrella and keep cool.' 'You should always try to show a cool demeanour before your employees.' 'Cool' also implies 'lack of interest'. 'We were received very coolly at their house.' 'Cool down' implies 'becoming or making cool'. 'Though she gets agitated soon, she also cools down soon.'

cortage/cortege

'Cortege' which means 'a train of attendants' or 'a procession' is the correct word, not cortage.

council/counsel/consul

'Council' and 'counsel' possess the same pronunciation. A 'council' is 'a ruling or a managing body'. 'I am one of the members of the City Council.' 'Counsel' means 'advice' or 'guidance' or 'direction'. 'Your counsel is required by us for guidance and to take better decision.' 'Consul' means 'an agent appointed by a government to reside in a foreign land to discharge certain administrative duties'. 'Mr. Kumar has been appointed as a Consul to Egypt to work in the Indian Embassy to take care of important matters.'

couple/couple of

The term 'couple' means 'pair' 'combine' or 'team'. But as a phrase the use of 'couple of' is quite distinct. 'A couple of distinguished guys were invited to attend the ceremony.' It means a small number of important guys were invited.

credible/credulous/incredible

Many people are often confused about these three words. 'Credible' implies 'believable' or 'trustworthy'. 'Credulous' means 'naïve' or 'unsuspecting' or 'innocent'. 'He made a credible speech that convinced all.' 'He looks quite credulous by his simple demeanour (though he may not be so simple).' 'The story he narrated was quite incredible (hard to believe).' His performance on (the) stage tonight was 'incredible'. It would mean that his performance was excellent.

criteria/criterion

'Criterion' which means 'standard of judgement', is a singular noun. 'Criteria' is its plural form. 'The judges at the fancy show had no criteria to select the right persons.'

cost/cost of/at all cost

'Cost' indicates 'price'. It is not used in a passive voice. 'The cost of this item is only $10.00.' 'Cost of' implies in relation to 'risks and expenses'. 'Although we won the case, the 'cost of' losing our seat in the council was colossal.' 'At all cost' implies 'at the loss or expenses'. 'They should reach the destination at all cost.'

crucifiction/crucifixion

The correct term is 'crucifixion' and not 'crucifiction'. 'Jesus Christ was certainly crucified, so cruci+fiction is not acceptable.'

cry/cry out

'Cry' means persons, animals or birds 'making sounds expressing feelings of pain and fear'. 'When I take him to school every morning, he cries bitterly.' 'Cry out' implies 'crying until one gets emotional relief.' 'Let her cry out until she feels relieved.'

currant/current/currently

'Currant' is a kind of fruit cultivated mainly in California. 'Current' implies 'present times'. We also use the term to denote electric 'current'. 'Currently' is an adverb and 'current' is adjective. 'She is likely to visit us in the current month.'

D

damped/dampened

The term 'damped' implies something which is 'moist' or 'humid' or 'wet'. Dampened implies 'to be wet'. 'When you walk through a river or when it is drizzling, you get dampened.'

dare/dare to

'Dare' is used primarily in negative sentences, including those with *hardly, never* and *no one*. It unfolds some kind of doubt. 'Dare' also implies the meaning 'of being brave enough'. It also suggests courage. 'I dare say you would never like to see him again.' However, when we add the preposition 'to' after it, it simply adds some 'stress' to highlight the situation. 'Don't you dare to repeat this mistake again!' 'No one dares to approach the boss to request him for one day's leave.'

data/datum

Both 'data' and 'datum' have to do with 'information' or 'statistics' or 'facts' or 'figures' or 'numbers'. Data is used either in a singular or plural form depending on the intention of the user and keeping in view the context. The use of datum is not very common in English these days.

deep-seeded/deep-seated

The correct form is 'deep-seated' which means that something like 'a feeling is deep seated within'. 'A feeling of hatred is deep-seated in her heart against the unusual environment of the college.' There is nothing like deep-seeded which some people may say while they talk without being aware of the fact that it is wrong to say like that.

defence/defense

The term 'defence' is an English version but 'defense' is an American version, both meaning the same.

definite/definate

'Definite' is the only correct spelling of the word; not 'definate', which people sometimes use by mistake. 'I am definite that she will definitely come to see me.'

defuse/diffuse

The term 'defuse' means 'to rescue' or 'to smooth out'. 'She defused the tense environment of the house by her kind demeanour and compassionate outlook.' 'Diffuse' means 'to spread' or 'to distribute something out'. 'His kind smile diffused throughout the environment and made the audience feel good.'

degrade/downgrade/denigrate

'Degrade' means 'lower in rank or status'. It has to do with real 'reduction in value' and not with 'insult' which is implied in the term 'denigrate'. 'Downgrade' means 'lowering in grade'. 'The teacher was so strict with his students that he downgraded each and every student in the class if they made even a single mistake.'

dieties/deities

When we refer to gods we mean 'deities'. 'Dieties' is a wrong use of the term by the people who get confused.

deny/refuse

Most people get confused about these two terms. 'Deny' means 'to refute' or 'to contradict'. 'He denied the charges against him.' 'Refuse' means 'to say no' or 'to decline' or 'to turn down'. 'I refused to go to the market along with him.'

depends/depends on

While people converse, they may use the term 'depends' but in writing it is advisable to use 'depends on'. 'It depends on your advice what my next move will be.'

depreciate/deprecate

'Depreciate' means actually 'to reduce or to decrease in value'. But if one deprecates something, he/she is keeping a low opinion about it. 'The share prices depreciated a lot last month without any serious reason.' 'I deprecate that the share prices would go very low this month.'

desert/dessert

Some people get confused about the spellings as well as pronunciation of these two words. 'Desert' is a stretched wasteland full of sand. 'Dessert' is a sweet dish which often people like to eat at the end of a meal or whenever.

device/devise

Like the terms 'advice and advise' these two terms 'device and devise' are also confused to spell correctly. 'Device' means 'a tool or an instrument'. 'A screwdriver is a device to undo or to do a screw.' 'When you devise (work out) a plan to do something, only then you can find out whether the device is likely to work or not.'

dialate/dilate

'Dilate' means 'open' or 'widen' or 'expand'. 'When the doctor put some medicine into my eyes two or three times, in a few minutes the pupils dilated.' However, 'dialate' is not a correct term. The spellings of the two words are so close that people often get confused.

die/die from/die for/die hard

The term 'die' has several uses in English language. 'Die' means 'a block of hard metal with a design', cut in to use for shaping coins, medals, etc. It also means 'to come to the end of life'. 'Die for' means 'to sacrifice oneself for someone or for some purpose'. 'A good soldier will never hesitate to die for his country.' 'Die hard' implies to die only after struggle. 'He died hard but to reveal any secrets against his country.'

different than/different to/ different from

Both 'different to' and 'different from' have no difference in meaning except that one is an American and the other is a British (different to) expression. However, 'different than' is used by a few whose grip on the language is not as strong.

For example, 'The way she smiles is different than (from) her sister's way of smiling.'

dire straights/dire straits

When one is passing through a dangerously narrow path or tracking through hard times, one may say, 'I am in dire straits these days.' However, the term dire straights, is a misuse in English.

disburse/disperse

'Disburse' means 'to distribute' something especially money among people. 'Please disburse this amount among the labour.' 'Disperse' means 'to scatter' or 'to leave'. 'The labour dispersed after they received their wages.'

disc/disk

As far as modern technology is concerned, 'disks' usually reproduce data magnetically, whereas 'discs' reproduce data optically with the help of lasers.

discreet/discrete

'Discreet' means 'prudent' or 'careful' or 'tactful'. 'Discrete' means 'separate' or 'distinct' or 'detached'. 'She is very discreet in her relationship with her boss.' 'She keeps herself discrete as far as the office politics is concerned.'

discussed/disgust

The meaning of 'disgust' is 'loathing' or 'less liked' or 'repulsion'. 'His way of expressing things was quite disgusting today.' But 'discussed' is simply the past form of the verb 'discuss'. 'They discussed the plan at length before executing it.'

disinterested/uninterested

These two terms are quite confusing and often people mix up when using them. When a person is bored with something he/she may be 'uninterested' in it. But when one is 'disinterested' in something, it would mean he/she is 'neutral' and 'unattached' to it in any way.

dissent/descent

'Dissent' means 'holding an opinion which differs from others'. 'Many people held dissenting views against the Managing Director's opinion.' 'Descent' means 'going or coming down'. 'There is a steep descent down the mountain to the village below.'

divide up/divide into/divide on

'Divide up' implies 'to separate' or 'to break up'. 'Could you please divide up the work before you start it?' 'Divide into' is used as, 'Please divide Rupees Ten into three persons equally.' 'Divided on' is used as: 'We are not divided on this issue.'

doctorial/doctoral

The term 'doctoral' is related to the word doctor and is often misspelled and mispronounced as 'doctorial' .

documentated/documented

The correct form is 'documented' which means 'acknowledged' or 'accepted' or 'standard'. 'Documentated' is a wrong term for it. 'The article you wrote was well documented.'

dominate/dominant

'Dominant' is an adjective which means 'leading' or 'foremost' or 'principal'. 'Dominate' is a verb and can be used as, 'He dominated during the entire meeting by his aggressive manner and unusual conduct.'

doubtlessly/doubtless

The word 'doubtless' is an adverb and so is 'doubtlessly'. It is good to use 'doubtless' when required rather than 'doubtlessly' although this term is also not incorrect and can be used sparingly. 'It is doubtless that she will show up tonight at the theatre.' 'She will show up at the theatre doubtlessly.'

dove/dived

'Dived' is a past tense of 'dive', but many people (mostly Americans) like to use 'dove' as the past tense of 'dive'. 'She dived into the pool from a great height.' 'Dove' is also a wild pigeon.

dreamt/dreamed

Both the terms are common in use and possess the same meaning. They are used as the past tense of the term 'dream' (noun) when it is used as a verb.

dribble/drivel

'Dribble' means a 'trick' or 'drip' or 'leak'. 'Drops of water are dribbling from this small hole.' 'A good football player knows how to dribble his ball.' When one does not like someone's speech and desires to condemn it, one may use the term drivel. 'His manner of speech and the content, was absolutely drivel.'

drier/dryer

Please use a 'dryer' to make the clothes 'drier'.

drive/drive hard/drive at

'Drive' means driving or being driven (not in a public vehicle). 'Driving hard' implies 'to put pressure on someone'. 'You are driving me hard in that case.' 'Drive at' implies 'intent'. 'What are you driving at after reading the report?'

drownding/drowning

'Drownding' is not a correct word but 'drowning' is correct and indicates to 'getting suffocated or submerged in water'.

dual/duel

These two words are also often miss-spelt and people get confused about their meanings. 'Dual' implies 'double' or 'twin' or 'twofold'. 'She has a dual role in that particular movie.' 'Duel' means 'contest' or 'fight' or 'gunfight' or 'combat'. 'Both the boys ultimately had a duel when they came out of the class after the school was over.'

dyeing/dying

'Dyeing' means to change the colour of a cloth with the help of some kind of dye. But 'dying' implies when someone has stopped taking breaths any more.

E

ease/at ease/ease off

The simple meaning of 'ease' is 'freedom from work or discomfort or trouble or anxiety'. 'He leads a life of ease.' 'At ease' conveys a sense of 'to be relaxed'. 'Please stand at ease.' 'Ease off' implies 'to give relief'. 'Can I ease you off your current problems?'

e.g./i.e.

When one means (in writing) 'for example', one can use 'e.g.', but if one means to state 'that is' one should use 'i.e.' Both the terms have been taken from the Latin phrases.

e-mail/email

The term 'email' is commonly used in ordinary correspondence. Some people like to use the term as 'e-mail'.

eager/anxious

Some people intermix these two terms considering that they mean the same. But there is a subtle difference in their meanings and use as well. Suitable examples can perhaps clear the misunderstanding. 'I am eager to meet him once again.' It would mean I am 'looking forward' to meet him again. But if you say, 'I am anxious to meet him again', it would imply 'some sort of worry is implicit' on your part in meeting him.

ect./etc.

'Etc' implies *et cetera* which originates from Latin, meaning 'and others'. Currently 'etc' is less in use.

either are/either is

In English language, the second noun in a sentence carries the number (singular/plural) of the verb. So, if one uses 'either' with 'are' it has to have the subject or the second noun in plural. 'Either she or they are in a hurry.' 'Either she or her friend is in a hurry.'

embaress/embarrass

In fact, 'embaress' is a wrong word. Some people use it erroneously in place of 'embarrass' which means 'humiliate' or make 'uncomfortable' or 'make shy'. 'You embarrassed me by your uncanny conduct.'

embedded/imbedded

Proper spelling of the right term is 'embedded', which means 'rooted' or 'set in' or 'implanted'. 'Goodness is embedded in his character.' 'Imbedded' is more or less not used for it.

emigrate/immigrate

The word 'emigrate' means 'to leave a country'. 'My neighbours have emigrated (moved out) to England.' 'My neighbours have immigrated (come in) here from France.'

eminent/imminent/immanent

'Eminent' means 'prominent' or 'famous'. 'Pt. Nehru was an eminent person.' 'Imminent' means 'pending' or 'in the offing'. 'The court's decision is imminent in his case.' 'Immanent' means 'remaining within' or 'taking place within the mind'. 'The effects of his father's death are quite immanent.'

empathy/apathy

'Empathy' implies containing 'similar feelings' or 'appreciative perception'. 'My friend was quite empathic about my lecture that I delivered in the college this afternoon.' The term 'apathy' is almost opposite to sympathy. It means 'indifferent' or 'lack of concern' or 'lack of interest'. 'The man who was sitting by your side while I was delivering the lecture seemed to possess some sort of apathy towards my delivery.'

endnotes/footnotes

'Endnotes' are the notes given at the end of a chapter by a writer to highlight the point of reference. 'Footnotes' are provided by a writer just at the foot of a page to explain some special point that has occurred within that page.

endquote/unquote

'Endquote' is a redundant term while 'unquote' is often used by a speaker during a conversation when he does not want to provide details about someone or something. It is also used by an author when he intends to close (end) a quotation.

enquire/inquire

Some people often confuse about these terms but both the words have the same meaning. 'Enquire' is more common with the British, while 'inquire' is commonly used in the US. However, both are acceptable at either of the places.

enter/enter into/enter on (upon)

'Enter' means 'to come or to go into'. 'The President's car has entered the parade ground.' 'Enter into' means 'to begin' or 'to open'. 'When I entered into the conversation, the atmosphere had already cooled down.' 'Enter on' means 'make a start on (upon) a new career'. 'She entered on a new job today.'

envelop/envelope

'Envelop' is a verb and can be used as, 'She enveloped (enclosed) the gift in a bright paper.' 'Envelope' is a noun which means 'a covering for a letter'. 'I need an envelope for my letter.'

epitomy/epitome

'Epitome' means 'essence' or 'embodiment' or 'personification'. 'St. Teresa was an epitome of purity, spirituality and goodness.' However, epitomy is not a correct expression.

every (as singular/plural)

'Every' is used both in singular and plural forms. It depends how one uses it. 'Everyone was present in the party.' 'Everyone who attended the party brought gifts for each other.'

everytime/every time

The term everytime is incorrect. It has two separate words — 'every time'.

evidence to/evidence of

The standard expression is 'evidence of' rather than 'evidence to', which is not much in use. Except when we say: 'She gave an evidence against the culprit in the court, when she was summoned by the judge', it is hardly used in written English. 'Her keeping quiet before the judge for a long time is an 'evidence of' her incapability and a sign of ignorance as well.'

exacerbate/exasperate

Though both the terms look quite alike, but they are not. Their meanings are also different. 'Exacerbate' means 'to increase the feelings of bitterness' or 'to aggravate'. 'Her rough tongue exacerbated (increased bitterness) her father's feelings.' 'Exasperate' means 'to infuriate' or 'to annoy' or 'to frustrate'. 'His unwelcoming conduct, exasperated (led to frustrate) me.'

exaggerated/over-exaggerated

When something is 'exaggerated' it is already stretched. Therefore, over-exaggerated is redundant and superfluous.

exalt/exult

'Exult' means 'to triumph' or 'to take pride'. 'She exulted to learn that her son stood first in the final examination.' 'Exalt' means 'to elevate in rank, status, power, etc.' 'He felt exalted by his sudden promotion.'

excape/escape

There is no term like excape. 'Escape' means 'to run away' or 'run off'. 'The thieves escaped from the police custody.'

exceed/accede

'Exceed' means 'go beyond' or 'go above'. 'Sometimes you exceed the driving limit imposed by the police.' 'Accede' means 'to agree' or 'to give consent'. 'I acceded finally to her request.'

excess/in excess of/ to excess

'Excess' implies 'fact of being or amounting to be more than expected or not proper'. 'Your excessive involvement in extracurricular activities is affecting your studies.' The bus conductor said, 'Sir, your luggage is in excess of twenty pounds.' 'To excess' means 'to an extreme degree'. 'When his father died, he carried his grief to excess.'

excuse/excuse for/in excuse of/excuse from

'Excuse' means 'reason given to explain or defend one's conduct'. 'Please excuse me for my rough conduct.' 'Excuse for' implies some sort of 'false moves or acts'. 'She always makes excuses for coming late to the school.' 'Excuse from' means 'free from a duty or requirement'. 'You are excused from attending the meeting.'

exhileration/exhilaration

'Exhilaration' is a noun which means 'high spirits' or 'excitement' or 'happiness'. 'As soon as his team scored the fifth goal, he was full of exhilaration.' However, the term exhileration is a wrong word mistakenly taken by some for 'exhilaration'.

expecially/especially

'Especially' is often mispronounced as 'expecially' which is a wrong word.

expresso/espresso

The correct term is 'espresso' used in relation to when one makes a coffee with the pressure of steam. 'Expresso' is an incorrect term.

F

fable/fabled

'Fable' is 'a legendary story of supernatural happenings' or it is 'a narration to teach a lesson'. 'Fabled' implies 'fictitious' (created or untrue) told or celebrated in fable'. 'My grandmother always created fictitious stories parallel to fables to teach me moral precepts.'

fabulous/incredible

'Fabulous' means 'wonderful' or 'magnificent' or 'great'. Anything which is positively captivating and which is liked by the human sight or mind could be 'fabulous'. One can say, 'The sight of the river flowing between the hills is so fabulous that I don't feel to stop looking at it.' However, 'incredible' means 'unbelievable' or 'farfetched' or 'absurd'. But the term is used to express something unusual. For example, 'The story of the movie was so incredible that I watched it very attentively.' In this case, the term 'incredible' would mean 'very captivating and unbelievably good'.

face/face to face/save face

'Face' means the front part of head that includes eyes, cheeks, mouth, etc. But when it is used as a verb it means 'to withstand'. 'Can you face her crying so bitterly?' 'Face to face' implies bringing two persons (parties) confronting each other. 'It would be better if they come face to face and discuss their problem.' 'Save face' would mean 'to refrain' or 'to avoid'. 'He avoided visiting the club last night to save his face from the impending charges of corruption against him.'

fair/fare

The meaning of 'fare' is to 'go' or 'travel' 'or 'get along' or 'succeed'. 'She fared well in the examination.' It also implies 'paying the price charged to transport someone'. 'I paid $ 20.00 for the taxi fare.' 'Fair' means 'pleasing in appearance' or 'just' or 'conforming to the rules', etc. 'The principal was quite fair (just) in distributing the scholarship money to the needy students of his school.'

fall/fall down/fall short/fall flat/fall out

'Fall' means 'act of falling'. 'Be careful lest you should fall from the cycle.' 'Fall down' means 'to be shown to be false or inadequate'. 'Due to your improper conduct, you have fallen down in my views.' 'Fall short' implies 'not going far enough'. 'He fell short of his mother's expectations.' 'Fall flat' means 'fail to have the desired effect'. 'His advice fell flat as it did not have intended effect.' 'Fall out' means 'going off parade' or 'happen'. 'It so fell out that he could not reach the station to see them off.'

far/far from/far off

'Far' indicates 'a great distance'. 'He travelled very far.' 'Far from' is used to indicate 'instead of'. 'She is far from satisfactory as far as her demeanour is concerned.' 'Far off' implies 'far away'. 'They will reach Paris in a few hours though it is a far off distance from here.'

far and few between/few and far between

The correct phrase 'few and far between' is mistakenly used as 'far and few between' by some people. 'There are few and far between chances that he would show himself today.'

farther/further

Some people consider these two terms as equal but there is a slight difference in their use. 'Farther' has to do 'with physical distance'. 'He lives farther from here.' 'Further' refers to the 'extent of time or degree'. 'If you go further back in time you will find that history does not provide us much.'

fatal/fateful

When death or accidents are involved we use the term 'fatal'. But when no casualties are involved we use 'fateful'. Although our car met an accident, no fatal casualties occurred. Only some people were hurt, but it was a 'fateful' incident.

fearful/fearsome

When we use 'fearful' we mean we become 'afraid of' or 'frightened of' something. 'Fearsome' means 'terrifying' or 'alarming' or 'terrible'. 'He looked so ugly and fearful today that I did not like to look at him.' 'Total silence without any movement in that forest was very fearsome.'

few/little

'Few' means a 'small number of' or 'hardly any'. 'We possessed only a few dollars when we went to the restaurant.' 'Little' means 'tiny' or 'minute' or 'small'. 'There is little sugar in this pot.' 'This boy is little in size.'

finish/finish up/finish off

'Finish' means 'bring or come to an end'. 'He has not finished his assignment yet.' 'Finish up' means 'completing a task or finishing eating' etc. 'Please finish up your dinner soon.' 'Finish off' means 'kill' or 'destroy'. 'The great loss he sustained in the business last year nearly finished him off.'

fiery/firey

'Fiery' originates from 'fire' and 'firey' is not a correct form.

first come, first serve/first come, first served

In fact, the phrase 'first come, first served' is in tune as it means 'if you come first, you will be served first.' Therefore, 'first come, first serve' is not acceptable as it conveys a different meaning.

fiscal/physical

'Fiscal' has to do with 'finances' and matters related to 'budgeting' whereas 'physical' has to do with 'body' related matters. It also refers to 'corporal'. Therefore these two words are quite different and should be used carefully without any confusion.

flair/flare

'Flare' implies 'in flame' (noun), or 'blazing' (verb). 'When she listened to his talk she 'flared up'(burst into anger).' 'Flair' implies 'style' or 'elegance'. 'When I looked at her this morning she was quite in flair.' 'She has a flair for acting.'

flammable/inflammable

Both the terms mean 'easy to catch fire'. Therefore one should not get mixed with the spellings. 'This box possesses inflammable (flammable) material, so handle it with care.'

flaunt/flout

'Flaunt' means 'to show off' or 'to display'. 'You flaunt your taste in sports by participating in all the possible events that normally no good sportsman can do. 'Flout' has to do with 'disobeying' or 'ignoring'. 'When I asked him to complete the assignment, he just flouted.'

flesh out/flush out

The police 'flushed out' all the criminals from the county (district) last night. It means the criminals were driven out by the police. 'Flesh out' implies 'to give shape to'. 'The artist fleshed out the sketch so beautifully that it looked as if it were real.'

flounder/founder

'Flounder' means 'great struggle'. 'When people are in trouble they flounder to come out of it.' It is something like when one is in water and about to drown but struggles hard to save himself/herself. 'Founder' means 'to fill with water and sink'. 'He foundered hard to get out from his problems.' But it means he could not save himself and lost or drowned into the problems. Thus, these two terms which look identical are quite different in meaning and spellings as well.

flustrated/frustrated

'Frustrated' means 'upset' or 'disturbed' or 'annoyed'. 'I was just frustrated to see him in a shabby school dress.' 'Flustrated' is not a correct form to be used for 'frustrated'.

for free/free

In fact, 'for free' is an acceptable term and is more commonly used than simply using 'free'. The ice-cream is 'for free' at the end of the dinner.

for one/for one thing

'For one' is a short form used by some people 'for one thing'. For example, 'For one, I wish to visit the museum is that it contains certain unusual specimens of animal bones, that I have never seen before.' Therefore, 'for one' implies 'for one thing' or 'for one reason' as well.

for sale/on sale

When one sells something it is 'for sale' but when prices of things are reduced, they are 'on sale'. You can observe a sign of 'on sale' in different kinds of stores, especially when seasons change in a year.

forbidding/foreboding/formidable

'Forbidding' implies 'frightening' or 'hostile' or 'grim' or 'unfriendly'. 'The way that man walks he looks forbidding.' 'The sky looks forbidding as if very soon a fierce storm is bound to follow.' 'Foreboding' means 'ominous'. It also implies 'apprehension'. 'Early rains in this season are foreboding. They may bring good harvest.' 'Formidable' means 'tough' or 'alarming' or 'dreadful'. But lately it is also used to show compliments. 'John is the only boy who looks formidable to compete with you in music competition in the class.'

forceful/forcible

'Forceful' implies 'powerful'. 'Forcible' implies 'use of power'. 'The impact of his speech was quite forceful.' 'The police forcibly entered into the house and caught the culprit.'

forego/forgo

'Forgo' implies to 'go without' or to 'do without'. 'I had to forgo my claims on the property on compassionate grounds.' 'Forego' is a commonly used word which also implies 'give up' or 'do with out' or 'pass by'. 'Fore' means before. It is therefore used with the terms like 'foregoing conclusions' etc.

foreword/forward/forwards

The terms 'forward' and 'forwards' have no difference in meaning and application, as both mean 'ahead' or 'front-wards'. A 'foreword' is written for a book highlighting its main items or indicating certain characteristics of the author.

forsee/foresee

'Foresee' implies 'to look into the future'. 'I could foresee the result of his ill-deeds.' 'Forsee' is not a correct form.

fortuitous/fortunate

'Fortuitous' events happen all of a sudden by chance. 'My uncle's sudden visit was purely fortuitous for me.' 'I was fortunate (lucky) to see my uncle after so many years.'

foul/fowl

If someone goes against the rules in a game he commits a 'foul'. A chicken is a 'fowl'.

fulsome

'Fulsome' is a phrase that many people may take to mean as 'wholehearted' or 'generous'. But on the contrary it may mean as 'disgusting' or 'excessive' or 'immoderate'. When it is used with words like praise as 'fulsome praise', it means 'excessive praise'. 'Fulsome praise' may also mean flattery on the part of the person who makes a 'fulsome praise' for someone.

G

gaff/gaffe

Since these two words have almost identical pronunciation and are not far off in spellings, many people get confused in their use. 'Gaff' means 'a strong hook with a handle used for landing large fish'. It also means 'a cheap place for entertainment'. 'The captain can handle the gaff very comfortably if he likes.' 'Some people love to visit a gaff on Saturday evenings to enjoy there.' '*Gaffe*' is a French word which means an 'embarrassing mistake' or 'an awkward act'. People should not mix it up with gaff.

gamut/gauntlet

'Gauntlet' means 'a metal glove to protect the hand or wrist'. 'Gamut' means 'the whole range or scale of something'. Both the words are quite different in meaning but sometimes people are mixed up in using them.

Gandhi/Ghandhi

The correct spelling of Mahatma Gandhi's name is Gandhi and not Ghandhi.

gaurd/guard

'Guard' is the correct spelling of the term, not gaurd.

gear/gear up/gear down

'A toothed wheel as a part of a machine to connect the engine' is known as a 'gear'. A gear helps the driver to put the engine in different positions to make it run at different speed.' 'Gear up' or 'gear down' means 'change up and down' or 'adjust one thing to the working of another'. 'You should gear up your economic status to stand at par with the other businessmen in the market.'

get/get done/get about/get along/get away

'Get' means 'to become or to pass from one state to another'. 'Very soon you will get used to the cold weather of this place.' 'Get done' means 'to complete something'. 'She may get her assignment done by the next Monday.' 'Get about' implies 'be no longer confined'. 'This important news will soon get about.' 'Get along' means 'manage'. 'I can get along with her even though she is often aggressive in her behaviour.' 'Get away' implies 'managing to leave'. 'She finally got away with my valuables as soon as she got a chance.'

go a long way/go very far/go along with/go down

'Go a long way' means 'a considerable contribution towards something'. 'My advice helped him a lot as it went a long way to improve his finances.' 'Go very far' implies 'to last'. 'Your misconduct will not help you go very far in life.' It simply means that your bad habits will not help you to progress in life but may ruin you ultimately. 'Go along with' means 'to accompany' or 'agree with'. 'He did not go along with me smoothly after one month's friendship.' 'Go down' means 'to sink' or 'be swallowed'. 'This drink is so bitter that it would not go down my throat.'

gibe/jive

'Gibe' implies 'taunting' or 'mocking' at. 'Jive' means 'a fast lively music' and also the 'dance' performed with this music.'

gig/jig

In fact, the term 'jig' is used in a phrase like 'the jig is up' which means 'the game is over' or 'nothing is left any more'. 'Gig' implies 'a rapid dance' or a' piece of music with rapid beats'. A 'gig' is a device with four hooks to hook the fish through their body and also a long light ship's boat.

gild/guild

An organisation like a theatre or comprised with professionals is known a 'guild'. When an object is coated with gold, is known as 'gilded'.

god/God

'God' is the Almighty, only One, Who is omnipotent, omniscient, and all pervading, while gods with a small 'g' is an indicator of all the other gods and goddesses.

grammer/grammar

The correct word is 'grammar' which is often misspelled as 'grammer'.

grateful/greatful

The right word to show gratitude or 'feel obliged' is 'grateful' and not 'greatful'.

gratis/gratuitous

The term 'gratis' implies when 'a good act is done without getting any payment'. 'One would say, it is just gratis.' Such an act if done in a way which is uncalled for is 'gratuitous'.

grisly/grizzly

'Grisly' means 'gruesome' or 'horrible'. 'One should abstain from doing grisly acts.' A 'grizzly' is a bear.

ground zero

'Ground zero' indicates the point which is the centre of the impact of a nuclear bomb.

H

hairbrained/harebrained

'Hairbrained' is commonly misused for 'harebrained', which means 'silly as a hare' or 'crazy', which is the right word and is used in writing. 'He is a harebrained kind of a person.'

hangar/hanger

Clothes are hung on a 'hanger', while a plane is parked in a 'hangar'.

harbringer/harbinger

A 'harbinger' is 'a forerunner' or 'a herald' or 'a messenger' or a 'bearer of news'. 'Harbringer' is an incorrect term used for harbinger.

hard disk/floppy disk

A 'hard disk' is a high capacity storage device like the main disk inside a computer. A floppy disk is a three and a half inch diskette used to copy and store data from the computer.

hardly/hardly ever/hardly never

'Hardly' means 'barely' or 'scarcely'. 'I can hardly reach the railway station on time today.' 'Hardly ever' is the right expression and not 'hardly never'. 'I can hardly ever do that job for I have no interest in it at all.'

hardy/hearty

'Hearty' is often misused as 'hardy' which altogether has a different use. When one says she is 'hale and hardy', one means she is fine. 'Hearty welcome' or 'hearty sendoff' are the right expressions to be used at the occasions concerned.

heading/bound

It is appropriate to use 'heading south' or 'heading north' and also proper to say: 'Northbound trains are running late today'. 'Heading' simply means 'route' or 'direction' and may imply the meaning 'leading' or 'moving to'.

hear/here

'Hear' has to do with your ear and 'here' means right 'at this place' or 'at this point'. 'I could not hear what you said a minute before.'

heared/heard

'Heard' is the past tense of the verb 'hear' and heared is an incorrect expression.

heartrendering/heartrending

When one's heart is touched by some grim happening, we may say, 'It was a heartrending (touching) incidence'. Sometimes people misuse for it the term 'rendering' which is not appropriate.

heighth/height

'Height' is the correct expression not heighth which sometimes people use for height due to confusion.

heroin/heroine

'Heroin' is an addictive drug extracted or made from opium but 'heroine' is the term used for a leading lady character in a movie.

highly looked upon/highly regarded

The term 'highly regarded' implies 'given great respects'. It is incorrect to use 'highly looked upon' for it. Her conduct is excellent so she is 'highly regarded' by her employees.

hippy/hippie

'Hippie' is indicative to a long haired and often aimlessly roaming person but when we say he is 'hippy' we mean he has 'wide hips'.

historic/historical

'Historic' may mean related to history or very old, but the more appropriate term for something which is famous and old too, is 'historical'. 'At Sikandra, near Agra, there is a historical building that contains the Emperor Akbar's tomb.'

HIV virus

The full term is 'human immunodeficiency virus' (HIV). Since virus is already referred to in 'HIV' it is a mistake to add virus after HIV virus.

hoard/horde

'Hoard' means to 'store' or to 'accumulate'. 'Horde' implies a herd of animals or a mob of people. Someone who accumulates treasure is a hoarder and his/her treasure thus hoarded is his/her 'hoard'.

hold/ahold

'Hold' means to 'retain' or 'clutch' or 'grip' or to 'cling to'. 'He held the books in his right hand.' 'Ahold' is not a correct term.

hold breath/hold it down/hold out/hold up

'Hold breath' implies 'holding breath when there is fear or excitement'. 'Hold it down' means 'to keep it down or keep under'. 'The finance minister has been trying hard to hold the prices down.' 'Hold out' means 'above' or 'offer'. 'As he has been working very hard, it holds out some hope for success.' 'Hold up' implies 'delay'. 'We were held up at the railway station for a few hours due to rains.'

holistic/wholistic

'Holistic' is the correct term which means 'related to the complete system and not to its parts'. It is a 'holistic' picture of the company where you are working currently. The term 'wholistic' is incorrect.

how come/why/what happened

'How come' is a casual expression of 'showing a bit of surprise' as well as it is a casual expression to 'express a little concern'. 'Why' is a formal expression to put 'query'. Similarly 'what happened' is a way of expressing concern and questioning to know all about the matter.

howsomever/however

'However' is the correct expression which sometimes people mix up with an incorrect term, 'howsomever'. 'However' is a kind of expression that often comes in the beginning of a sentence or while starting a new clause after the principal clause, showing change of mood, concern, contradiction, or something of that nature'. 'I know that you all will join the marriage of my friend. You also expect me to come there as already promised. However, I may now come there only after you reach the friend's place as I have some additional assignments to finish.'

hypocritical/showy

'Hypocritical' implies 'conduct' or 'speech' intended to make one 'appear good or true when one is really not so'. 'Showy' implies to be 'gaudy' or 'flashy'. 'Some people feel happy in being showy as they suffer from complexes.'

hysterical/hilarious

'Hilarious' has to do with 'to be funny or showing off happiness', while 'hysterical' conveys the sense of someone 'having a fit of hysteria'. 'The lady in the hospital looked quite hysterical as her conduct was not normal.'

I

idea/ideal

A thought or a notion is an 'idea'. When people practise best ideas, they become 'ideals' of many.

if/whether

Although both 'if' and 'whether' possess almost identical meanings and are used in similar situations, 'whether' is more formal and is used in speech when people have two different or comparable situations. 'She will like to join the club whether you like it or not.'

if I was/if I were

In traditional English, expressions denoting conditional future, such as, 'If I were a king (If I was a king), I would have made her my queen', is a valid expression. So also at times 'was' can be used in place of 'were'. Otherwise, normally 'were' is always used with a plural subject in simple past tense.

ignorant/stupid

'Ignorant' means 'not in the knowledge of certain facts'. But being 'stupid', means possessing mental deficiencies. 'I was ignorant about his latest publications.'

illicit/elicit

'Illicit' implies 'illegal' or 'unlawful' or 'dishonest'. 'It was an illicit act on his part to commit theft at his friend's house.'

'Elicit' means to 'draw out' or to bring out' or 'to extract'. 'I can elicit his true intentions out of this letter.'

impertinent/irrelevant

'Impertinent' means 'insolent' or 'impudent' or 'impolite'. Though it is not in common use these days for it is a term which is quite hurting, most people like to use 'irrelevant' instead. 'What he talked to me was all irrelevant', which means he talked to me things of 'unrelated' or 'inappropriate' nature.

imply/infer

In fact, both the terms are very near as far as their meanings are concerned. However, you use 'imply' when something is being suggested to you without being stated clearly. 'Inference' is made when one is trying to reach a conclusion based on some proofs. 'You can infer what he intends to do from what we know about him so far.'

in another words/in other words

The phrase 'in another words' is not correct, which is confused with the right phrase 'in other words', which is often used 'when after telling something for a long time the speaker wants to conclude those things in a nutshell.' He says, 'In other words, what I mean is this.'

in depth/indepth

'In depth' is the correct term and 'indepth' is often misused for it by mistake.

in fact/infact

'In fact' is the right usage and not 'infact'.

in lieu of/in light of

'In lieu of' implies 'instead of' or 'in place of'. It is the right expression. 'In light of' is an incorrect expression. 'She thanked me profusely in lieu of awarding me for the work.'

in to/into

Both the prepositions have different uses in English language. 'We all went 'into' the theatre at the right moment. Later on she came 'in' 'to' tell us that she too was joining us.' Mark 'in' and 'to' in the second sentence. These two words have a different use to perform in different situations. Hence they are different from 'into'.

incidence/incidents

Both the words are so close in pronunciation and meaning that often they are confused during conversation. 'Incidence' means a 'happening' or an 'occurrence'. 'That incidence took place late at night.' 'Incidents' is a plural form of 'incident' which also means 'occurrence'. 'Last night several incidents of theft happened on this road.'

incidently/coincidently

'Incidentally' is used to reflect something additional that the speaker has just thought. For example, after a long discussion one of the speakers reflects: 'Incidentally, a new thought has just come to my mind.' 'Coincidentally' means 'something happening at the same place or at the same time'.

'Coincidentally, my cousin also arrived home at the same time when I entered the house.'

indepth/in depth

'In depth' has two words not one. So 'indepth' is an incorrect term. 'She went quite in depth to know her subject.'

individual/person

People, at times, use correctly the term 'individual' when they don't mean to refer someone particularly. It indicates a casual use of the term. 'Each individual in the team must abide by the rules.' When you use the term 'person' you intend to stress on 'individual' more. 'Each person must report to me at the right time.'

in fact/infact

Like 'in depth', the term 'in fact' also has two words, not one. Therefore, 'infact' is a wrong use of the term. 'In fact, I wanted to know her intentions clearly so I visited her second time.'

infinite

The term 'infinite' means something which is 'never ending' or 'endless' or 'countless' or 'unlimited'. 'The sky is infinite.' But sometimes it is also used to convey something in billions or in 'a very great number'. 'There were infinite people to receive their leader at the railway station.'

inquire about/inquire after/inquire into

'Inquire about' implies 'ask for information about' or 'find out'. 'Could you please go to the inquiry and inquire about what time the next bus leaves?' 'Inquire after' means 'ask about'. 'I wish to inquire after my wife's health.' 'Inquire into' implies 'try to learn the facts about'. 'You need to inquire into the matter immediately.'

install/instil

'Install' means to 'fit' or 'put in' or 'fix'. 'I am going to install Tata's satellite dish at my place.' 'Instil' means to 'inspire' or 'fill' or 'implant'. 'Her emotional talk instilled great hope in me.'

instances/instant

Any sort of examples given mean 'instances'. 'While narrating the facts about her life, he quoted many instances that showed her strong will and clean of conduct.' 'Instant' means 'immediate' or 'at the spot' or 'direct'. 'While I was talking about my friend, he appeared at the instant.'

intense/intensive

Some people at times get confused when they use these two words which though look similar in meaning, but they are not. 'Intense' is an adjective which means 'strong' or 'powerful' or 'forceful'. 'She embraced me with intense love.' 'Intensity' is a noun which means 'strength' or power'. 'She reflected a great intensity of love when she hugged me.' 'Intensive' is derived from 'intensity'.

interface/interact

'Interface' implies 'border' or 'boundary' or 'line'. 'Interface is a computer term used to connect two things.' 'Interact' means 'interrelate' or 'act together' or 'work together'. 'When you connect a computer with Internet, it interacts and connects you to a great network.'

internet/Internet

'Internet' means the network people connect to. The term needs to be capitalised. Thus, it is the most correct use of it.

interpretate/interpret

'Interpret' means to 'take' or 'understand' or 'take to mean'. 'I could interpret the letter correctly.' 'Interpretate' is a wrong term often confused for interpret.

ironic/sarcastic

The appropriate meaning of the term 'ironic' is 'mocking' or 'sarcastic' or 'odd' or 'peculiar'. Not every ironic comment made by someone is sarcastic, which basically means to 'mock at or to hurt.' 'Ironic' is related to something 'peculiar', which happens when we don't expect it.

irregardless/regardless

'Regardless' is the correct term which sometimes is misused by some when they say 'irregardless' which is an incorrect use for it. 'Regardless of my repeated requests, she did not attend the party.'

its/it's

'Its' is a possessive pronoun relating to 'it' or 'itself', while 'it's' implies 'it is'.

J

jealous/envious

Both the words have the same meaning except that there are hidden meanings behind them. One becomes 'jealous' of someone when one's girlfriend tries to become friendly to some other boy, but one can be 'envious' to one's own friend when he/she has scored more marks in examinations.

jewellery/jewelry

'Jewellery' is the correct term and a British spelling. Some people mix it up with 'jewelry', which is an American spelling.

join/join hands/join in

'Join' simply means 'put together' or 'unite' or 'connect'. 'Will you please join these tables with the others?' 'Join hands' imply to 'combine in an enterprise'. 'Please join hands with me in this project.' 'Join in' means 'to come into the company' or 'be a part of it'. 'Can she join in on the dinner table?'

judgement/judgment

'Judgement' is a British spelling which is still popular in certain parts of the world but Americans have dropped 'e' from it after 'g'. Thus it becomes 'judgment'.

K

keep

'Keep' means 'cause to remain'. 'Please keep this change.'

keep back/keep away/keep down/keep off/keep up/ keep out

'Keep back' implies 'not letting others to know about it'. 'Could you please keep back the secret?' 'Keep away' means 'preventing from going'. 'Keep away from his company.' 'Keep down' means 'hold in subjection'. 'The culprit was kept down in the police custody overnight.' 'Keep off' implies to 'remain at a distance'. 'Will you please keep off from the stove?' 'Keep up' imply to 'go forward at the same pace' or 'speed up'. 'Walk quickly so that you can keep up with others.' 'Keep out' implies to 'remain outside'. 'Keep out of their plans for you may be involved with problems.'

kick

'Kick' means 'act of kicking'. 'He kicked the ball so hard that it fell into my neighbour's yard.'

kickback/kick off/kick against/kick out

'Kickback' implies 'percentage of payment made' to one who has been instrumental to make money by right or wrong means. It is a kind of bribe money. 'In corrupt countries, even senior government officials are used to accepting kickbacks.' 'Kick off' implies 'starting a game'. 'The minister kicked off the ball to start the game.' 'Kick against' means to 'show annoyance'. 'I kicked against his advice for in my view it was not fruitful.' 'Kick out' means 'to expel' or 'dismiss'. 'As the student misbehaved in front of the principal, he was kicked out by him.'

kick-start/jump-start

Motorcycles start with a 'kick-start'. When your car battery is dead it is connected with another fully charged battery. Then by connecting the charged battery to your dead battery through a cable you give a 'jump-start' to your dead battery.

kind/kind of

The standard expression is 'kind of' and not ' kind'. 'I haven't seen that kind of a thing before.'

knock

'Knock' means 'gust' or 'waft'. 'When the lights were off last night, I heard a knock at my door.'

knock down/knock out/knock about/knock up

'Knock down' means 'striking to the ground or floor'. 'When she was standing near her house, a motorcyclist knocked her down.' 'Knock out' implies 'defeat of a player by the other one'. 'The Indian wrestler knocked out the American wrestler in the freestyle wrestling.' 'Knock about' means 'leading an unsettled life, moving from place to place'. 'Paul has knocked about throughout the country but he is still unsettled.' 'Knock up' means 'waking up'. 'Please knock me up at six in the morning tomorrow.'

L

laissez-faire

'Laissez-faire' is a French expression. It indicates to 'a doctrine opposing governmental control of economic matters beyond that necessary to maintain peace and property rights'. It also simply means, 'let do'. At times during conversation people sometimes use this term which may indicate 'indecisive' or 'not indicating clear intentions' or 'inform'. If we say 'That man is a kind of laissez-faire', it may mean that he has no clear position to reflect on certain importance issues.

lamblast/lambaste

'Lambaste' implies to 'excessive beating, not actually blasting'. 'Lamblast' is an incorrect expression used for lambaste. 'The captain of the ship lambasted some of the sailors for impropriety.'

lapse/elapse

Both the terms have originated from Latin, mean 'to slip' or to 'elapse' mostly referring to the passage of time. 'Lapse' normally implies to a 'change of state'. 'The date for changing the oil in your car has lapsed.' 'A lot of time has elapsed (gone) since we last visited your mother.'

last name/family name

In fact, 'last name' and 'family name' may not be different but to avoid any confusion it is better to say 'given name' and family name.

later/latter

'Later' means 'afterwards' or 'in a while'. 'See you later on.' 'Latter' refers to the 'last item' out of (mainly from) two'. While you are involved in conversation with someone you may say, 'Which of the places would you like to visit first this morning, the Taj Mahal or the Badkal Lake?' And the reply comes, "The 'latter' one, please."

lay/lie

These two words are often confused by many people. When one is tired one wants to 'lie' down on bed. 'Lay' is past tense of lie. 'Lie' also means relating to something which is 'not true' or something which is 'false'. 'She is used to telling lies about herself.'

leach/leech

'Leach' implies 'leak' or 'filter' or 'seep'. 'A good soap can leach the dirt out from the clothes.' 'Leech' is a 'blood-sucker' mostly found in dirty or low water ponds. It is also sometimes used to indicate 'sucking' of something. 'Your brother is constantly leeching off money from your pocket on flimsy grounds.'

leant/leaned

Both 'leant' and 'leaned' are past-tense of the verb 'lean' which means 'to incline' or 'bend from a vertical position or in a particular direction'. It also means to 'depend on'. 'When her friend visited her last evening, she suddenly leant (leaned) toward the pillar standing in the middle of the hallway.' 'Can I lean on (depend on) you when struck up with financial problems?'

leapt/leaped

Both the terms are past-tense of the verb 'leap' which means 'to spring through the air from one point or position to another' or 'to move quickly and lightly'. 'My brother suddenly leapt from his chair and landed on the floor.'

leave

'Leave' means 'to go away from'. 'Leave me alone right now.'

leave for/leave alone/leave over

'Leave for' implies 'to go away to'. 'She is leaving for school in a few minutes.' 'Leave alone' means 'not to interfere with'. 'Please leave that man alone.' It would mean don't tease him or disturb him. 'Leave over' means 'to postpone something'. 'I would advise you to leave over your decisions for some time.'

legend/myth

'Legends' refer to famous deeds of people, 'like legends of Sri Ram'. A 'myth' is generally a traditional story which is important as it is significant in some way. It is quite customary to use the term 'myth' to indicate 'a fantasy' in common usage.

lend/loan

In the olden days in U.K. 'lend' would mean 'to give something to someone on loan' for some time. Perhaps the sense of taking it back was implied in lending. 'Can you lend me your cycle right now?' Americans use 'lend' for 'loan' which is now a more accepted term for 'loan'. 'Please lend me some money today.'

lense/lens

'Lens' is now an (American) accepted term for lense. It means 'a curved piece of glass or plastic' used singly or combined in an optical instrument for forming an image.

less/fewer

'Less' pertains to 'amount', and 'fewer' to 'number'. 'I have less money to give you than what you have asked me for.' 'I have a fewer number of pairs of shoes than what you have.'

let

'Let' means 'allow to'. 'Let me go right now.'

let it be/let it go

'Let it be' implies 'to be permitted' or 'to be quiet' or 'unworried'. 'Let that man be there for some time.' 'Let it go' means 'to release one's hold on'. 'Please let the ball go.'

liable/libel

'Liable' means 'legally responsible' or 'accountable' or 'answerable'. After the death of his parents 'I am liable to take care of his interests.' 'Libel' means 'defamation' or 'slander'. If someone defames you with false charges, he 'libels' you. Both these terms are sometimes confused and used for the other.

library

At times some people drop one 'r' from the term and pronounce it as 'libry' which is incorrect.

lighted/lit

Both the terms 'lighted' and 'lit' are past-tense of the word 'light' and are often confused.

lightening/lightning

'Lightning' is the correct term used for the 'bright flashes in the sky during a cloudy storm'. 'Lightening' means to 'make something lighter'. The young man helped in lightening the old man's burden.'

like/as if/like for

The terms 'like' and 'as if' are synonyms but at times they are used at different occasions. For example, 'She walked in the party as if she was (were) a queen.' 'Use of 'as if' is more customary in formal English than the term 'like', which is often used in conversation. 'He brags like a rich man.' It means he is not rich but he talks like that. Use of 'for' after 'like' is redundant.

literally

'Literally' is often used to denote 'actually' or 'factually', but often people misuse it. It needs to be used only to distinguish between a figurative and literal meaning of a phrase. "Whatever I have said so far, 'literally' it means this..."

little/few

'Little' refers to amount and 'few' to number. There is 'little' milk in the container. I have a 'few' pennies in my pocket.

look at/look back/look good/look about/look down/look forward

'Look at' means 'to use one's sight' or turn the eyes in some direction'. 'Look at' these pictures. How pretty are they! 'Look back' implies 'looking at angrily'. She looked back at me instantly after she heard my reply. 'Look good' means 'being attractive' or 'looking beautiful'. You 'look good' today. 'Look about' means 'be on the watch'. Are you still 'looking about' for a good job? 'Look down' implies 'despise' or 'consider others inferior'. Some rich always 'look down' upon the poor. 'Look forward' means 'anticipate'. She is 'looking forward' to see me soon.

look over/look through/look well

'Look over' means 'to inspect'. 'Let us look over the papers once again carefully.' 'Look through' means 'to revise' or 'to examine'. 'You should look through these bills before you pay them.' 'Look well' gives the sense of 'being healthy in appearance'. 'You look so well today.'

lose/loose

Perhaps these two words are confused due to mispronouncing the term 'lose', which should have 'Z' sound in it when spoken. Please don't let 'loose' your cat for you may 'lose' it forever.

lose ground/lose heart/lose sight/lose track

'Lose ground' means 'no longer in a winning position'. 'She lost grounds in the legal case as her arguments were poor in the court.' 'Lose heart' means 'to get disappointed' or 'to lose courage'. 'He lost heart to know his final examination result.'

'Lose sight' implies 'fail to take account'. 'The police lost sight of the criminal after a long chase.' 'Lose track' means 'fail to hear'. 'The newsreader was so fast in his speech that I lost track of most of the important news today.'

lustful/lusty

Some people sometimes get confused with these two words that look quite close in meaning but they are really not. 'Lustful' implies 'filled with sexual desire'. 'My friend looks quite lustful today.' 'Lusty' implies 'full of vigour and good health'. 'The lusty young man is the owner of a health club.'

make

'Make' means 'construct' or 'produce' or 'frame'. 'Please make a cup of tea for me.' 'The school has made certain rules to protect its children.'

make it from/make-believe/make out/make sense/ makeshift/make after

'Make it from' means 'producing by combining materials'. 'Wine is made from grapes.' 'Make-believe' means 'to pretend' or 'pretence'. 'Let us make-believe that we are rich instead of poor.' 'Make out' implies 'deducing'. 'I cannot make out anything from your comments.' 'Make sense' implies 'to provide meaning'. 'Her promise does not make any sense for she has been telling lies even before this.' 'Makeshift' means 'for time being until better arrangement is made'. 'Please use this small bed as a makeshift arrangement until a better bed is provided.' 'Make after' means 'to pursue' or 'to chase'. 'She made after the thief as if she were a policewoman.'

mantle/mantel

'Mantle' means a 'layer' or a 'blanket' or a 'covering' or a 'cloak'. 'She often wears a mantle whenever she visits a holy place.' A shelf above a fireplace is known as 'mantel'.

many/much

'Many' implies with 'numerous' or 'loads of' or 'several', and 'much' indicates 'quantity' or 'amount' or 'a great deal'. 'There are many brave people who have made history of this country.' 'There is nothing much to look at this picture.' 'We cannot do much for him now.'

marital/martial

'Marital' refers to marriage and 'martial' relates to war. 'What is your marital status? Are you yet married or unmarried?' 'The Chinese are good at martial art.'

marshall/marshal

'Marshal' is the correct term. A very senior and experienced person is appointed as the Field Marshal in a war. Often people get confused with marshal and use marshall instead.

mass/massive

'Mass' and 'massive' are often confused by people for they look having identical meanings. But their meanings as well as their applications are different. 'Massive' means 'bulky and heavy'. 'It's a massive structure of a building.' 'Mass' means 'a body of coherent matter usually of indefinite shape' or 'bulk in size and number'. When we refer to 'masses', we mean 'a great number of assembled people'. 'A great mass of people assembled at the funeral of the Senator.'

masseuse/masseur

'Masseur' is a person who practises massage. 'Masseuse' is the term used for a female who practises massage.

mathmatics/mathematics

'Mathematics' is the right word, not mathmatics.

may/might

Both these terms are used interchangeably, but 'might' possesses somewhat lower likelihood than the term 'may' which suggests more possibility. For example, 'She might come tonight, and she may come tonight', can clarify the difference.

mean time/meantime

'Mean time' is the correct use of the term not 'meantime'. Such subtle differences must be kept in mind to avoid mistakes.

medal/meddle

The term 'medal' is self-explanatory, while 'meddle' means to 'interfere' or to 'intrude'. 'You don't need to meddle in other's affairs.'

mettle/metal

'Mettle' means 'courage' or 'bravery' or 'spirit'. Some people have extraordinary courage and can display their 'mettle' at any time. 'Metal' is a kind of solid substance usually hard and shiny.

media/medium

Television is a visual and audio 'medium'. The term 'medium' implies 'means' or 'vehicle' or middle' or 'average', etc. Newspapers are both, a broadcast 'medium' as well as a 'media'.

mediocre

The simple meaning of the term is 'average' or 'medium' but it is often used to denote a more negative sense. 'He is just a mediocre student.'

memento/momento

A 'memento' is a 'souvenir' or a 'token' or a 'keepsake'. The guests were presented 'mementos' at the end of the party. The word 'momento' is incorrect to use for it.

memorium/memoriam

'Memoriam' is related 'to be retained in one's memory' and therefore, memorium is a wrong use for it.

metaphor

'Metaphor' is a 'symbol' used in written English to highlight some image or to indicate an allegory.

minature/miniature

'Miniature' (not minature) is the correct word, which means 'small' or 'tiny' or 'minute'. 'This map is the 'miniature' of the bigger one hanging on the wall.'

mischievious/mischievous

'Mischievous' is the correct term which means 'naughty' or 'playful' or 'roguish'. 'Your little son is quite mischievous.' The word 'mischievious' is an incorrect word used sometimes by mistake for 'mischievous'.

moral/morale

'Moral' refers to 'ethics' or 'ethical' or 'good' or 'decency'. 'Precepts are mostly based on morals.' 'Morale' refers to 'self-esteem' or 'spirits' or 'confidence'. 'A military personnel has to keep his morale always high to fight against the enemy.'

moreso/more so

Like the term 'mean time', 'more so' should be spelled as two clear words and not compressed in one as 'moreso'.

Ms

'Ms' indicates a gender and is used instead of 'Miss' or 'Mrs'. When S is used in capital after M as 'MS', it refers to 'manuscript' or 'an academic degree' also.

much differently/very differently

We all behave 'very differently' in different circumstances. We 'much differ' in our opinions sometimes.

murmer/murmur

'Murmur' means 'speak softly'. 'The noise coming out of this brooklet is just like a sweet murmur.' 'Murmer' is an incorrect spelling of 'murmur'.

mute point/moot point

A 'moot point' may be a point worth discussing at a meeting. 'Mute point' is a misuse of the term 'moot point'.

myriad of/myriad

'Myriad' implies 'a lot of'. I have a lot of work to do. 'I have 'myriad' duties to discharge tonight.' To suffix 'of' after it is redundant.

N

naïve/nieve

The term 'naïve' is referred to someone who is 'inexperienced' or 'immature'. My friend Pradeep is quite 'naïve' in household matters. 'Nieve' is an incorrect term used for 'naïve'.

nauseous/nauseated

'Nauseated' means a 'feeling to vomit'. Correct usage is 'nauseated' and not 'nauseous' which sometimes people use by mistake. 'I am nauseated and I feel like vomiting', is the correct way of expressing that your stomach is upset and you feel to vomit.

neice/niece

Some people get confused with 'niece' and mispronounce it as neice. A niece is a daughter of one's brother or sister, or a daughter of wife's brother or sister.

nip it in the butt/nip it in the bud

'Nip in the bud' is the correct phrase which sometimes some people express as 'nip in the butt' by mistake or deliberately. It simply means that 'the progress in work was stopped'.

no sooner when/no sooner than

The correct usage is 'no sooner than' and not 'no sooner when'. 'No sooner had she arrived at the railway station, than the train steamed in.'

none/no one

'None' and 'no one' are also sometimes confused. 'No one' is an expression to denote a singular number. 'No one of you is leaving this place until I permit.' 'However 'none' can be used as a plural term too. 'None of us are hungry right now.'

nonplussed

'Nonplussed' implies the sense of being 'confused' or 'baffled' or 'puzzled'.

'Looking at his awful physical condition after the accident, I was totally nonplussed.'

not hardly/not at all

Some people may use 'not hardly' as a slang instead of 'not at all'. In formal English people often use 'not at all'. 'Would you mind sitting in this chair?' The reply comes: 'Not at all'.

nuptual/nuptial

'Nuptial' is related to 'marriage' or 'wedding' or 'matrimonial'. 'All the advertisements on this page are related to nuptials.'

O

observe/observed with

'Observe' means 'watch carefully'. 'Please observe her behaviour carefully.' 'Observed with' refers to 'occupy the mind with'. 'I observed with distress how she suffered with pain.'

offense/offence

'Offence' is commonly a British term and 'offense' is American, both meaning 'crime' or 'wrongdoing' or 'evil doing'. 'If you drive recklessly and hit someone by your vehicle, it is an offence.'

okay/OK

Both 'OK' and 'okay' are very popular in most of the established languages of the world and convey the same meaning i.e. 'all correct' (*oll korrect*).

old fashion/old-fashioned

'Old-fashioned' is the traditional spelling of the term, which means 'keeping in view the conventional and age-old traditions in thought and in practice'. 'She still holds old-fashioned views about solemnising a marriage.' 'Old fashion' simply refers to 'an old fashion' and does not convey the meaning that 'old-fashioned' does.

on accident/by accident

At times things or events happen 'by accident' without your desire or efforts. 'On accident' does not convey that sense and is not a correct term to be used for 'by accident'.

'It was just by accident that I reached her place although I was looking for a hotel to pass the night.'

on to/onto

Sometimes people interchange both these terms. But 'on to' are two separate and correct words which are used in situations such as, 'He travelled on to his house just to show him the right papers.'

once and a while/once in a while

The correct term is 'once in a while' not 'once and a while'. 'You visit me only once in a while (sometimes) these days.'

one in the same/one and the same

'One and the same' is the traditional phrase which means 'they all are alike'. 'You cannot count upon these boys much as they are one and the same as far as their working philosophy is concerned.' 'One in the same' is, at times, used for 'one and the same' mistakenly.

only

Often people misuse 'only' by putting it at a wrong place in a sentence in written English. It should go only before the word or phrase it modifies. 'I shall tell you everything only when you promise to keep all that with you.'

oppress/repress

Both these terms don't convey exactly the same sense though their meanings are not very far from each other. That means they convey varied sense. 'Oppress' means 'keep down' or 'subjugate'. 'Administrators who oppress their subordinates are like dictators.' 'Repress' simply means 'to keep under control'. 'The police repressed the rioters in half an hour only.'

ordinance/ordnance

'Ordinance' means 'decree' or 'order' or 'rule'. 'Ordnance' means 'weapons' or 'artillery'. 'The Government passed an ordinance for security reasons that all the citizens would carry their identity cards with them when they travelled out of their towns.'

Oriental/Asiatic/Asian

An 'Asian' is a person hailing from East or South or Central Asia. An 'Oriental' is now often taken to be an 'old-fashioned' term for an Asian or hailing from that region, and most people don't like to be addressed that way. 'Asiatic' is neither a customary nor a preferred term used for an Asian.

orientate/orient

'Orientate' is an English term meaning to 'familiarise' or to 'orient' or to 'adjust'. Americans prefer to use 'orient' instead of 'orientate'. 'The new teacher first orientated all her students about her background before she started teaching formally.'

ostensively/ostensibly

'Ostensibly' means 'apparently' or 'supposedly'. 'Ostensively' is a wrong term used for 'ostensibly'. 'She looked apprehensive quite ostensibly.'

outlet/plug in

There is a plug at the end of this cord which can be 'plugged in' (to) the 'outlet' attached to the wall of the kitchen.

over-exaggerated/exaggerated

If one exaggerates something it is already over-stretched. Therefore, there is no need to prefix 'over' before the term exaggerated. It would be incorrect if you do so.

overdo/overdue

The payment of electricity bills is 'overdue' now as the last date for the payment is already gone. One should not 'over do' anything as its results will always be bad. At times 'overdo' is also used to convey sense of 'showy conduct'. 'It is often seen that when he starts praising his son, he overdoes it.'

oversee/overlook

'Overlook' implies 'forgetting something'. 'Oversee' implies 'watch over' or 'administer' or 'manage'. 'Could you please oversee the marriage arrangements to-night?'

P

pair

The word 'pair' is used in singular number mostly, such as 'This is a pair of glasses.' 'It is a nice pair of shoes.'

palate/palette/pallet

These three terms are often likely to be confused on account of their spellings and more due to their pronunciation. 'Palate' has to do with one's 'taste' and it is the 'roof of one's mouth.' A 'palette' is a flat board on which a painter mixes paints. A 'pallet' is 'a bed' or a 'platform which holds goods or on which goods are kept.'

parallelism

When phrases in a series, one after the other, are separated by a comma and have the same sort of grammatical forms, they are known as parallelism. For example, 'She wanted to become a doctor, be a great practitioner and help her people in the village she lived.'

parallelled/paralleled

The correct spelling of the word is 'paralleled' not 'parallelled'.

parameters/perimeters

A 'parameter' is commonly used for 'a mathematical constant', or 'characteristic of something'. 'When we say perimeter of something, we mean its boundary.' The words are often confused because of their spellings which fall so near. In order to avoid confusion, let us keep in mind one correct spelling, such as 'parameter'.

parentheses

Most people make mistakes in using parentheses marks as they use them too much. They are required only when absolutely needed. Normally a sentence's final punctuation mark such as a full stop, exclamation mark or a question mark should go outside such a parenthesis, like (He... reached home safely).

parliment/parliament

The correct term is 'parliament' and not 'parliment'.

part

'Part' means 'separate' or 'divide'. Let us 'part' now.

part with/parting

'Part with' means to 'give up' or 'give away'. 'He is a great miser. He hates to part with his money.' 'Parting' implies 'departure'. 'Their parting very early today made us very lonely.'

pass/passed/past

If one is referring to time or distance one should use the term 'past'. If one refers to the action of passing, one needs to use 'passed'. However, passed is a past tense of 'pass' and can be used as: 'She could have passed the examination if she had worked harder.' Or 'She often passes in front our house without meeting us.'

pass away/pass on

'Pass away' implies someone 'dead'. 'My neighbour who was not very old, 'passed away' last night.' 'Pass on' means 'to give' or 'to deliver'. 'Please pass on this message to your friend when you see him next.'

past time/pastime

'Certain activity' with which one likes to involve 'passing the time' is his/her 'pastime'. When one uses 'past time' as two words, it refers to the time that has gone.

pay

'Pay' means 'wages' or 'salary' or 'money paid for regular service or work'.

pay back/pay off/pay out

'Pay back' means return that what one has borrowed. 'Pay me back the money you took from me last week.' 'Pay off' means 'to fulfil one's duty or obligations'. 'The master paid off the full wages to his servant at the end of the month.'

peace/piece

'Piece' means 'portion' or a 'bit'. 'Could you me give me a piece of bread please?' 'Peace' refers to mental 'tranquillity' or un-agitated mental state.

peak/peek/pique

'Peak' means 'climax'. 'A few years back Charleston Hasten was at the peak of his career.' 'Peek' means 'peep' or 'glance' or 'steal a look'. 'Pique' implies 'interest' or 'to attract' or 'to stimulate' or 'to wound the pride by harsh words'. 'When I invited her at the dinner she started uttering very unpleasant words as if she were piqued by my invitation.'

peasant/pheasant

A 'peasant' is 'a farm-worker', or 'a person engaged in agriculture'. 'Peasants' are an economically weaker class of people. A 'pheasant' is 'a kind of bird' or 'a game bird'.

peoples

During the Middle Ages the term 'peoples' was acceptable but now the term 'people' has been accepted as a plural form. However, if we still use 'peoples' it refers to 'the peoples' of different nations or different countries.

peremptory/preemptory

'Peremptory' means 'leaving no opportunity for denial' or 'imperative'. 'The witness presented such proofs against the culprit in the court that it made the judge's decision peremptory against him.' 'Preemptory' is a wrong spelling.

permiscuous/promiscuous

'Promiscuous' implies 'immoral' or 'loose'. It also implies 'relationships of two different kinds of individuals brought together to live'. 'When a male and female from different lands or places start living together without performing any formal rituals, their relationship can be taken to be promiscuous.' However, 'permiscuous' is a misuse of the term promiscuous.

pernickety/persnickety

'Pernickety' is an English word that means 'difficult to please' or 'fussy' or 'finicky'. 'Oh! My brother at times is pernickety.' 'Persnickety' has also the same meaning and is widely accepted in the US.

pick

'Pick means 'to take up' or 'remove' or 'pull away with fingers'. 'Pick' is also used to mean 'to start' or 'to indulge'. 'Please don't pick quarrels with your neighbours.'

pick at/pick off/pick out/pick up

'Pick at' means 'find fault with'. 'You always pick at others.' 'Pick off' means 'take' or 'pluck off'. 'The police picked off the criminal from the crowd.' 'Pick out' means to select carefully from a group of people or things. 'Today, she will pick out two students to lead the team.' 'Pick up' means 'to improve, increase'. 'The sales of gold ornaments will pick up during the marriage season.'

perogative/prerogative

'Prerogative' means 'privilege' or 'right'. It is often mispronounced and misspelled as perogative. 'A judge in a court has the prerogative to pardon someone's punishment if he/she thinks that the person has been falsely charged.'

perpetuate/perpetrate

'Perpetuate' means 'seeking to continue something'. 'The system perpectuated itself for several centuries.' 'Perpetrate' is related to the 'continued actions committed by the criminals.' It implies 'to carry out'(a crime).

perscription/prescription

'Prescription' is related to a doctor's 'instruction' or 'direction' or 'treatment'. 'Prescription' is the right word, but it is often mispronounced or misspelled as 'perscription'.

persecute/prosecute

When someone commits a crime, legal officers can 'prosecute' him/her. It means 'put on trial' or impeach' or 'take legal action'. 'Persecute' means 'hold' or 'harass' or 'hunt'. 'Please don't persecute him for he is not involved in any misdoing.'

personal/personnel

An individual has a 'personal' (individual or private) liking. 'This new company has a great number of personnel (employees) on its roster.'

personality

Simple meaning of the word 'personality' is 'character' or 'individual' or 'persona'. It is also used to identify show business 'personalities' as they are famous on the screen or famous as singers.

perspective/prospective

'Prospective' has 'to do with the future' or 'potential' or 'soon-to-be'. 'Your prospective bride along with her parents will be visiting us this evening.' While 'perspective' means 'vision' or 'sight' or 'viewpoint' or 'outlook'. 'From my perspective your decision to close that business is correct.'

peruse

'Peruse' means 'read thoroughly' or 'read in detail', but it is often misunderstood and is used to 'examine hurriedly' or 'check over hastily'. 'Please peruse these papers so that you may come to a right conclusion.'

phenomena/phenomenon

'Phenomenon' means 'fact' or 'occurrence' or 'observable fact'. 'Phenomena' is the plural term for 'phenomenon'. 'I hold that this phenomenon can be verified from other facts.'

picaresque/picturesque

A natural scene if it looks attractive and as lovely as a beautiful picture, is 'picturesque'. While 'picaresque' refers to literature involving a lovable rogue who wanders about just to have fascinating adventures.

picture/pitcher

Some people commit mistake in using these two different words because their spellings as well as their pronunciations are quite close but not exactly the same. 'A picture' should be pronounced as '*pikchur*' and the other word is pronounced as '*picher*'.

play

'Play' means 'to have fun' or 'pass the time pleasantly'. 'My son is playing in the living room.'

play down/play with/play up

'Play down' implies 'talk deliberately in such a manner so that he/she does not feel inferior to get support of others'. 'The boss is playing down with his employees so that they don't underrate him.' 'Play with' means 'to consider lightly'. 'It is not fair on your part to play with your friend.' 'Play up' implies 'to cause problems or pain'. 'I have joined the health club as my shoulder is playing me up again.'

playwrite/playwright

A 'playwright' is a person who shapes and fashions words into a dramatic form to create a proper effect on the audience. The word 'playwrite' is an incorrect term used mistakenly for 'playwright'.

plead innocent

The word 'plead' is connected with the term 'guilty' or 'not guilty' but not with 'innocent'. 'She pleaded not guilty in the court.'

please reply/please RSVP

RSVP is a French phrase meaning 'reply please'. So there is no use to suffix 'please' before it. It would be better to say, 'Please reply'.

point in time/point, time

The correct use would be 'at this time' or 'at this point'. Therefore both the terms 'point in time' and 'point, time' are redundant.

pole/poll

A 'pole' is 'a long stick', while 'poll' is related to 'survey' or 'census' or 'ballot'. 'One cannot make use of polls for each and every small issue to take public opinion.'

pompom/pompon

A 'pompom' is a kind of 'large gun'. The 'hairy ball' on the top of a knit hat is a 'pompon'. 'That colourful pompon looks very attractive on the hat of that sailor.'

populace/populous

If a country is crowded and full of population, like China or India, it is a 'populous' country. The population of a country may be referred to as that country's 'populace'.

pore/pour

The term 'pore' means 'a minute opening'. It also indicates 'scrutinising'. Did you 'pore' over the papers I gave you last night? 'Please pour (to send forth) some coffee in my cup.'

portentious/portentous

'Portentous' means 'ominous'. When people get confused they use portentious instead, but it is not a correct term.

portray/protray

'Portray' means 'display' or 'reveal'. 'Can you portray your paintings on this wall?' The word 'protray' is incorrect and often used for 'portray' by mistake.

possessed of/possessed by/possessed with

If someone owns a car, he/she is 'possessed of' it. If a ghost takes over someone's body, he/she is 'possessed by' it. If someone possesses a strong desire on account of some reason, we may say, 'She is possessed with a feeling of love for me.'

practice/practise

'Practice' and 'practise' both as a noun and verb respectively are acceptable in British English. But 'practice' is good both as a noun and verb in American English. However, the term 'practise' is not acceptable as a noun at either of the places. 'My doctor has a great practice for he practises twelve hours each day.'

practicle/practical

'Practical' is the correct term not 'practicle'. 'You may learn things when you involve 'practically' with them.'

pray/prey

Most people when in distress like to 'pray' to God. 'Last night a shopkeeper became the prey (robbed) of thieves.' 'A mouse is an easy prey (victim) of a cat.'

precede/proceed

'The term 'precede' implies 'to go ahead or before'. 'Proceed' means 'to go on'. 'My brother preceded me to the railway station.' 'Please proceed to the station as early as possible so that you may buy tickets.'

precedence/precedent

Both the terms look alike but they are not. 'Precedence' means 'priority' or 'preference'. 'My sister always gets precedence over me by my parents.' 'Precedent' means to set 'example'. 'If you don't punish the wrong person, you are likely to set a bad precedent for others.'

precipitate/precipitous

Both the terms are adjectives and mean 'impulsive' and 'steep' or 'abrupt' respectively. 'If one makes a precipitate decision, one makes an impulsive decision.' 'If you try to slide down the precipitious hill, you will go down sharply and may get hurt.'

predominate/predominant

'Predominate' is a verb and 'predominant' is an adjective. 'Predominate' means to 'prevail' or 'dominate'. 'Whenever she delivers a speech she predominates (prevails upon) others.' 'In general she is quite predominant (leading) than most of her friends.'

prejudice/prejudiced

'Prejudice' is a noun and means 'narrow-mindedness' or 'intolerance'. 'My friend's constant prejudice against me, made us part with.' 'I am still not prejudiced against him.'

premier/premiere

'Premier' has many meanings. It means a 'leader' or a 'head of state' or 'first' or 'leading' or 'foremost' etc. 'Tailor Woodrow was the premier road construction company in the whole of

West Africa during 1980s.' 'Premiere' means 'opening' or 'first night'. 'There will be a premiere show of Raj Kapoor's new movie, *Sangam*, on the coming Sunday night in the Bombay Talkies.'

premise/premises

A 'premise' is a term used in logic meaning 'something assumed while making an argument'. 'Premises' means a 'building' or 'location' or 'place'. 'This is my house and you are standing in my premises.'

prepone

'Prepone' means to 'move something earlier in time'. It is the opposite of postpone. But it is not a common term used throughout. Therefore, those who use it should be careful that the listeners understand the term.

prescribe/proscribe

'Proscribe' means to 'forbid' or to ban' or 'exclude'. It is just an opposite term to 'prescribe' which means to 'recommend' something. 'The doctors prescribe to take one aspirin every day with water and proscribe not to take it with tea.'

presently/currently

'Presently' means 'soon' or 'right now'. 'She may arrive here presently.' 'Currently' also means 'right now' but the term is used differently than 'presently. It may mean to 'indicate something that is happening right now'. 'They are fighting in the street currently.'

presumably/assumably

'Presumably' means 'most probably' or 'I presume'. 'Presumably she is in a right mood today.' In fact, 'assume' is the right term, which means 'to take for granted mostly without any proof'. 'Assumably' is not an accepted or a correct term.

preventive/preventative

Both 'preventive' (adjective) and 'preventative' (noun) may mean the same except that 'preventative' is an older term in use. 'Preventive' means 'protective'. 'Some doctors suggest certain medicines which work as 'preventives' (preventative) for certain diseases.'

principal/principle

Both these terms are often confused in writing. 'Principal' means 'first or highest in rank' or 'first'. 'She is the principal of this women's college.' 'Principle' means a 'precept' or a 'rule' or a 'canon'. 'Buddha concluded certain principles out of his deep reflections on the way of life.'

priority/prioritise

'Priority' means 'main concern' or 'precedence'. 'You must know your priorities in life'. 'Prioritise' means 'rank' or 'make a high priority'.

pronounciation/pronunciation

'Pronunciation' is the correct term meaning 'articulation' or 'accent'. 'Your pronunciation is absolutely distinct.' The correct spelling of the term is 'pronunciation'and not 'pronounciation' as often confused when writing it.

prophecy/prophesy

'Prophecy' is a noun which means a 'prediction'. 'Some learned astrologers can make very correct prophecies about a man's future.' 'Prophesy' is a verb. 'My astrologer always prophesies incorrectly.'

prostate/prostrate

'Prostate' is 'a gland' found in a man's body. 'Prostrate' means 'lying on the ground face downward'. 'Some people, when visiting a temple, prostrate before the idol of God.'

publically/publicly

'Publicly' means 'openly' or 'in public'. 'She confessed publicly that she went to see her friend twice last week.' 'Publically' is an incorrect term used for 'publicly'.

pull together/pull on/pull apart/pull out/pull over/pull through/pull up

'Pull' provides several meanings when suffixed with a preposition. 'Pull together' means 'work together'. 'All the workers are now pulling together.' 'Pull on' implies 'draw' or 'suck'. 'He is pulling on his pipe leisurely.' 'Pull apart' means 'to tear into parts'. 'The accident ridden car was pulled apart by the mechanic.' 'Pull out' means 'to move or row out'. 'The current of the river was very strong that the boat was pulled out into it by itself.' 'Pull over' means 'to steer to one side'. 'Will you please pull over your vehicle towards the red car?' 'Pull through' means 'to succeed averting difficulties.' 'Though she was so sick, she could pull through her ailment.' 'Pull up' means 'to improve one's relative state or condition'. 'I was able to pull up my studies just before the examinations began.'

purposely/purposefully

'Purposely' means 'deliberately' or 'on purpose'. 'He broke the rule purposely.' When people act keeping some specific purpose in mind, they act 'purposefully'.

put across/put aside/put away/put back/put down/put forth/put forward

Like the term pull, 'put' also provides several meanings when suffixed with a preposition or an adjective. 'Put across' means 'to communicate successfully'. 'A good teacher can always put across his ideas before the students.' 'Put aside' implies to 'lay down' or 'save'. 'I have put aside a good amount of money for my son's college education.' 'Put away' means 'to put in a storage', or 'to put in a usual place to save'. 'My father put my books away so that the rain could not destroy them.' 'Put back' means 'to return'. 'A good librarian always puts the checked in books at the right place.' 'Put down' means 'to land'. 'A good pilot can always put down his plane easily.' 'Put forth' means 'sending out'. 'The trees have put forth new buds after the autumn.' 'Put forward' implies 'to advance' or 'to put before the people for consideration'. 'The teacher put forward a new policy before his students for the home assignment.'

Q

queue/queer

'Queue' means 'line' or 'row'. 'Are you in a queue?' 'Queer' implies 'funny' or 'surprising'. 'He looks quite queer today.'

quiet/quite

The spellings of these two words are often confused by people. 'Quiet' means 'silence' or 'calm'. 'Please keep quiet in the library.' 'Quite' means 'fairly' or 'pretty'. 'I am quite well today.'

quotation mark

Often people put quotation marks (" ") around word or sentences denoting emphasis or to attract attention of the reader. At times too many quotation marks in a write-up may pollute the sense the writer wants to convey. Better avoid putting such marks to save the reader from confusion. For example, if someone writes, 'I met a few "educationists" last night in the meetings.' In that case the writer thinks that the educationists he met in the meeting were not real educationists but only so-called educationists. Therefore, one should use quotation marks only when one wants to highlight some point or an idea or a term or when he/she wants to quote (reproduce) exactly something written or mentioned by somebody else before.

R

racial/racism

'Racial' means 'ethnic' or cultural'. 'Some people don't easily give up their racial customs and traditions.' 'Racism' means 'racial discrimination or prejudice'. 'One, who keeps strong racial feelings, cannot be free from racism.'

rack/wreck

'Rack' means 'frame' or 'support'. 'Please keep the toys in a rack.' 'Wreck' means 'ruin' or 'destruction'. 'The divers are searching for the wreck of the ship deep in the sea.'

raise/rear

'Raise' means to 'lift' or to 'hoist'. 'The troops raised the flag after their victory.' The word 'raise' also means 'to bring up'. 'She raised her children with great efforts after her husband died.' 'Rear' means 'back' or 'stern' or 'bring up'. 'Her house is located in the rear row of these buildings.'

rapport

'Rapport' implies 'relationship' or 'understanding'. 'When people get along with each other in a very friendly manner they have good rapport.'

rather/sooner

'Rather' implies 'to a certain extent' or 'in some degree'. 'I would rather like to go with her than to wait here for hours.'

'I would sooner (earlier or quicker) like to accept her offer than to say no to her.'

ratio

We express relationship between one quantity and another by using the term 'ratio'. 'If there are 20 girls and 30 boys in a class the girls and boys ratio in the class would be 40% and 60% respectively.'

reach

'Reach means 'stretch to reach'. 'That pen is out of my reach.' 'Can you reach it?'

reach out/beyond reach/within reach

'Reach out' means 'to reach up to something'. 'Can you reach out to grab that book for me?' 'Beyond reach' implies 'out of one's reach'. 'I cannot reach that book as it is beyond my reach.' 'Oh! I can reach it. It is within my reach.'

reckon

'Reckon' means 'to calculate' or 'think' or imagine'. 'I 'reckon' you are not in a mood to visit your cousin right now.'

reckon in/reckon up/reckon on/reckon with

'Reckon in' means 'include or take into account'. 'Did you reckon in all the cost involved in making this furniture before selling it?' 'Reckon up' means 'to find the total of'. 'Please reckon up the hotel bill properly.' 'Reckon on' implies 'to base one's hopes on'. 'I very much reckon on your support.' 'Reckon with' means 'deal with' or 'settle with'. 'I shall reckon with this nasty servant after the party is over.'

reason/rationale/rationalisation

'Reason' means 'cause or motive or grounds'. 'The reason behind my supporting him is that he looks honest to me.' At times one also likes to explain the reasons for one's position or stand, and presents the 'rationale' behind it. The meaning of rationale is 'basis or foundation or the underlying principle'. 'When one tries to justify one's stand by giving false or lame excuses to make one's position look better before others, one is engaged in rationalisation.'

ravaging/ravishing/ravenous

'Ravaging' means 'devastating'. 'The invaders often ravage the towns they pass through.' 'It is often observed that enemy forces after their victory turn to ravishing (raping) the women.' 'At times, withdrawing forces after getting defeated become ravenous (extremely hungry or rapacious).'

reactionary/reactive

People often get confused about the use of these two terms. 'Reactionary' means 'desirous to prevent change and to maintain the present conditions'. 'Most Buddhists are turning reactionaries against the Chinese way of modernising Tibet.' 'Reactive' means 'tending to react'. 'When people act against the forced rule, the existing government often becomes reactive against those people.'

real/really

'Real' means 'genuine' or 'actual'. 'It is the real story of the poor man we met last night in the store.' 'Really' means 'actually' or 'in reality'. It provides more stress about something for which it is used. 'The food was really very good.'

rebelling/revolting

Both 'rebelling and revolting' mean the same. It means 'rising up' or 'insurgency against'. 'When Martin Luther King was murdered, people revolted (rebelled) against his murder.'

rebut/refute

There is a very thin difference in the meaning of these two terms. When one rebuts (confutes) an argument, one argues against it. But when one refutes (disapproves) an argument, one tries to prove it incorrect.

recent/resent

'Recent' means 'not long ago'. 'I have sent you the reply of your letter recently.' 'Resent' has two different uses with different pronunciation. 'I really resent ('*rizent*' meaning, feel bad) your way of concluding the argument.' 'I resent (sent again) the reply of the letter when the company said that they did not receive it.'

recognise/recognition

'Recognise' implies 'perceiving to be identical with something previously known'. 'After her long illness she has changed so much that I could hardly recognise her.' 'Recognition' implies 'perceiving something as existing or true'. 'His conduct was so kind that in recognition of it the people, who had gathered at the occasion, gave him a standing ovation.'

recreate/reinvent

'Recreate' implies 'reconstruction' or 'restoring'. 'Some people can recreate sounds like the cries of cats or dogs.' 'Reinvent' means to 'remake or reinvent something already invented'. 'The amateur scientist reinvented a new receiver which had similar functions as your radio has.'

recuperate/recoup

'Recuperate' implies 'getting over an illness'. 'My mother recuperated soon after her long sickness.' 'Some people believe in gambling to recoup (recover) their losses.'

recurring/reoccurring

'Recurring' means 'habitual' or persistent'. 'She gets recurring headaches these days.' 'Reoccurring' simply implies to occur (take place) again. 'The reoccurrence of the Moon's eclipse takes place when the Earth comes in between the Sun and the Moon.'

redundant/redundancies

'Redundant' means 'superfluous' or 'outmoded' or in 'disuse'. We have used this term at many places in this book indicating that certain words are now not in use so they are redundant. For example, the terms 'point in time' and 'point, time' are redundant. The correct use would be 'at this time' or 'at this point'. Similarly, spellings like colour and demeanour are redundant in American English. In their place the spellings they use are: color and demeanor. 'Redundancies' implies almost the same meaning as redundant but with a slight difference. Phrases such as 'free gift' or 'and plus' or 'end result' come under the category of redundancies.

reeking havoc/wreaking havoc

'Wreaking havoc' may simply mean 'intending or working great havoc'. 'The sudden rise in the petrol prices is wreaking havoc on our budgets.' 'Reeking havoc' is an erroneous term as reeking means smelling.

regard/regards

The correct terms are 'as regards' or 'in regard to' or 'with regard to', which can be used as: 'As regards your new proposal, I have not much to say. It seems pretty good.' 'In regard to our conversation held in my office on last Monday, I am not sure to say anything right now.'

regardless/irregardless

'Irregardless' is a redundant term often confused and used in place of 'regardless', which is already implicit with negativity. 'Regardless of his repeated requests, she skipped the party.'

regime/regimen

'Regime' and regimen' are very much synonym terms now and mean the same, such as: 'position of authority' or 'government in power' or 'course of treatment' or 'schedule' or 'procedure'.

In view of that, the use of the term(s) would depend on the context and intentions of the user. A doctor may say to the ailing person: 'Now onwards all what I have said to you is the regimen for you.' 'The present regime in the Centre is not serious to connect rivers with one another so that scarcity of water at remote places in the country may come to an end.'

regretfully/regrettably

Both the terms are synonyms and either of them can be used to introduce the feelings of 'regret'. However, it depends on how one uses either of them in a sentence. For example, 'Regretfully, (regrettably) our beloved mother passed away last night, as such the scheduled sports-meet is postponed until next week.'

reign/rein

A king reigns (rules or control) the state, while a horse rider reins his horse when needed.

relevant/revelant

'Relevant' means 'related or pertinent'. 'All what was discussed in the meeting was quite relevant to improve the tone of the school.' 'Revelant' is not a correct term and is often misused for relevant by mistake.

remember/remind

'Remember' means 'to have or keep in memory something that was said earlier'. 'I remember all what you told me two years back about her.' 'Remind' means 'to tell again about something or to do something. 'Please remind me to pay the workers' wages.'

remote/remotely close

'Remote' means 'distant or far-flung'. 'My village is in a remote area and very far from the main town.' 'Remotely close' is a incorrect combination of two opposite words — remote, which means far away, and close, that means near. It is just a wrong term to be used.

remuneration/renumeration

'Remuneration' means 'payment or wages'. 'The total remuneration you will get at the end of the week is Rs 20.' Some people on account of confusion use renumeration in place of remuneration by mistake.

repel/repulse

Both these terms are synonyms in meaning and in application. 'Repel' means 'to drive away' or 'to fight against'. 'Repulse' basically implies 'rebuff' or 'drive or beat back'. 'The enemy was repulsed (repelled) back.'

resister/resistor

One who resists something is known as a resister. 'A part of an electrical circuit is known as a resistor.' Both the terms are originated from the word resist which means 'oppose' or 'defy' or stand 'firm'.

respect/aspect

Both these terms are related as far as they refer to certain perspectives of an idea, but their meanings are not the same. 'In some respect whatever you have said so far, you seem to be right.' 'Considering all the aspects of this issue, I may think over again how to solve the problem.'

retch/detach/wretch

'Retch' means 'trying to vomit'. 'When your stomach is upset you like to retch.' 'Detach' means 'to separate or remove'. 'Please detach this tag from the box.' 'Wretch' means 'a miserable unhappy person'. 'He looks quite wretched today.'

reticent/hesitant

Both these terms look so alike but their meanings and applications are different. 'Reticent' implies 'reluctant to talk or reserved'. 'Why are you so reticent these days?' 'Hesitant' implies 'not willing to do anything being nervous or indecisive'. 'I am quite hesitant in joining the new company.'

revolve around/centre round

The two phrases can be used almost providing the same sense except that it depends on the speaker how he/she uses them. 'My total interest centres round the fact how you make money from the project.' 'Everything revolves around that one makes good profit from this project.'

revue/review

Both the terms look quite identical as far as their pronunciation is concerned but are different in meaning. 'Revue' refers to a 'variety show' on a stage, while 'review' refers to 'a write up one writes in a journal on in a newspaper indicating one's reactions about something published before.' 'Your review on my recently published article in *The Times of India*, was full of facts.'

ride

'Ride' implies 'to sit on a horse or riding a bicycle'.

ride in/ride on/ride out/ride down

'Ride in' implies 'be in and carried on'. 'I shall be riding in a car from the airport to home.' 'Ride on' implies 'to sit or go or be on'. 'She was riding on her mother's shoulders.' 'Ride out' means 'coming out safely through troubles'. 'We managed to ride out the storm.' 'Ride down' means 'chasing on a horse back, catch up with or to direct one's horse at someone to knock him/her down'. 'The police rode down fast and eventually caught hold the criminal.'

right/rite

In fact the word 'right' has several uses in English language. It means 'suitable' or 'privilege' or 'correct' or 'true' or precisely', etc. 'You asked him a right question at the right time today.' 'Rite' refers to a 'ritual or ceremony'. 'In a Hindu marriage several rites are involved.'

risky/risqué

Both the terms are quite identical as far as their pronunciation is concerned. '*Risqué*' which is originated from French, refers to an act 'daringly close to impropriety'. 'Risky' means 'involving risk'. 'His conduct was quite *risqué* last evening in the market.' 'It is quite risky to go out in the town at 12 o'clock in the night.'

rob/steal

Both 'rob' and 'steal' refer to two different kinds of acts. One who robs, he/she steals something. 'The thieves robbed the passengers and stole their money and gold.'

role/roll

A politician has a role (part) to play. 'When we go to Taco Bell, we eat a rolled up bean burrito.'

roomate/roommate

'Roommate' means sharing the same room with someone. It is the correct expression, not roomate.

root/rout/route

These three terms look alike when we speak them but their meanings and applications differ. 'Root' means 'origin' or 'cause' or 'basis'. 'The man in the red turban is the root cause of that skirmish.' 'Rout' implies 'disorder' or 'riot' or 'leading to disturbance'. 'People from both the communities went on arguing for a long time. It ignited routing.' 'Route' means 'way' or 'course' or 'path'. 'What route will you follow while going to Goa?'

rot/wrought

Both these words have almost identical pronunciation, but their meanings are wide apart. 'Wrought' means 'twisted or turned into different shapes'. 'The hammer-smith wrought the iron rod to give it an attractive shape.' 'Rot' means 'decomposed or rotten'. 'The entire food on the right table is a rot.'

round

The word 'round' has several uses in English language and many more when suffixed with a preposition or an adjective. 'It means 'go round'. 'Don't go round that table lest you should get hurt.'

round about/round off/round up

'Round about' implies 'not travelling by a shorter route'. It also refers to a circle situated at cross roads going in different directions. 'After listening to your travel plans I conclude that you seem to travel to the south of the country by a round about route.' 'Round off' implies 'to bring it to a satisfactory conclusion'. 'She rounded off her career by becoming a doctor.' 'Round up' implies 'bringing it to a whole number. 'The dealer rounded up the price of the car from 4 lakhs 20 thousand rupees to 4 lakhs only.'

run across/run after/run along/run away/run-down/run into/run off/run out/run over

The word 'run' has several uses when suffixed with a preposition or an adjective. 'Run across' implies 'pay a short informal visit'.

‘She ran across my house to borrow some money.’ ‘Run after’ means ‘try to catch’. ‘The police was running after the thieves.’ ‘Run along’ implies ‘to go away or be off’. ‘You better run along now.’ ‘Run-down’ means ‘looking weak or exhausted’. ‘You look quite run-down today.’ ‘Run into’ implies ‘meeting someone unexpectedly’. ‘I ran into an old friend while I was visiting the Annual Film Festival.’ ‘Run off’ means ‘stealing or taking away’. ‘The accountant has run off with important documents.’ ‘Run out’ means ‘come to an end’. ‘The provisions in the house are running out today.’ ‘Run over’ means ‘to review or recapitulate’. ‘Let us run over the notes again to build confidence.’

S

saccharine/saccharin

Though there is a little difference in the meaning of these two words, there is hardly any difference in their pronunciation. 'Saccharine' means 'nauseatingly sweet'. 'Saccharin' means 'a white crystalline compound used as an artificial calorie-free sweetener. 'Lesser poets at times compose saccharine sort of poetry.' 'I use one saccharin tablet every day with tea in the morning.'

sacred/scared

These two terms are quite apart as far as their meanings are concerned. 'Sacred' means 'holy or pure'. 'We always consider religious places as sacred.' 'The gods are sacred.' 'We are often scared (frightened) to go into the dark at night.'

sacreligious/sacrilegious

In fact, 'sacrilegious' implies 'an activity of committing theft of sacred property'. 'An amoral person only is involved in a sacrilegious activity.' 'Sacreligious' is an incorrect spelling used for 'sacrilegious'.

safety deposit/safe-deposit

Safe-deposit (box) is the correct phrase not safety deposit. 'People deposit their valuables in safe-deposit boxes in a bank.' Some people often get confused about the correct term and use the incorrect one by mistake.

sail/sale/sell

These three words, quite akin in pronunciation, often create confusion among some people. You 'sail' a boat, and someone may 'sell' eatables, drinks and coffee on it. Sometimes a few things may also be on 'sale' (deal or trade) on a boat.'

satellite

A few years back 'satellite' was a term indicating smaller bodies orbiting about planets, like the Moon. But it is more than a few decades now that artificial satellites are made by the scientists. These satellites are orbiting in the sky and helping our several systems, like televisions and information technology, to run efficiently.

save

'Save' implies 'making or keeping safe from loss, injury, etc.' 'A good doctor will always try hard to save his/her patient.'

save from/save up

'Save from' implies 'to keeping safe from injury or danger'. 'Can someone save that boy from drowning right now?' 'Save up' means 'to keep for future'. 'Wise people always save up for the rainy day.'

say/tell/express

'Say and tell' though convey the same meaning they are used slightly differently at times. 'When you casually converse, you 'say' things, but when you narrate, you 'tell' things.' You say, "Good morning! How are you?" Then after some time you start narrating (telling) many things. However, you 'express' an idea or thought either in writing or in speech.

scan/skim

It is quite surprising that recently 'skim' (to examine closely) is taken to be a synonym of 'scan'. Scan means 'to glance quickly' and it also implies 'to examine closely'. 'Please scan this document as quickly as you can.'

sci-fi/science fiction

'Sci-fi' is a widely used as a short-form for 'science fiction', which is objectionable to the science fiction writers who use SF instead. But SF is also taken to be a short-form of San Francisco. 'Currently in America Sci-fi is a science fiction TV channel, providing great entertainment to people.'

scrape

'Scrape' means 'to make smooth or level the surface by pushing a hard tool along with'. 'You need to scrape this piece of wood from both sides.'

scrape from/scrape out/scrape through/scrape together

'Scrape from' means 'to remove dirt, etc from'. 'Please scrape dirt from this floor.' 'Scrape out' means 'making by scraping'. 'Please scrape out all the filth from the kitchen.' 'Scrape through' implies 'just passed'. 'My daughter has just scraped through the examination.' 'Scrape together' implies 'to obtain by being careful or obtain with efforts'. 'The police scraped together some crowd when the minister arrived.'

scratch/itch

'Itch' is a tingling (tickly) feeling you like to 'scratch' (rub).

seam/seem

'Seam' means 'a line of stitching' or closure'. 'When two pieces of cloth are sewn together, a line is produced. It is called a seam.' 'Seem' is a verb, which means 'appear'. 'It seems that it will rain today.'

search/search out/search for

'Search' means 'to examine' or to 'look carefully'. 'She searched her room thoroughly to find out the ring.' 'Searched out' means 'look for' or 'examine carefully'. 'Please search out your own conscience carefully before passing judgements on others.' 'Search for' implies 'to find out' or 'to discover'. 'She is trying hard to search for the lost book.'

see about/see across/see around/see back/see off/see over/see through

When the word see is suffixed with an adjective or a preposition, it provides several meanings. 'See about' means 'deal with'. 'See across' implies 'guide' or 'to conduct' 'to help across'. 'Please help your brother to see across the floor lest he should fall down.' 'See around' means 'to say goodbye'. 'I would love to see him around.' 'See back' implies 'to accompany'. 'It is quite late in the night to see him back.' 'See off' means 'to say goodbye'. 'I am going to the airport to see off my brother.' 'See over' implies 'to visit and examine'. 'I shall see over the lot (piece of land) you wish to buy.' 'See through' means 'not to be deceived'. 'I can easily see through his dirty tricks.'

self-worth/self-esteem

'Self-worth' is not an appropriate term used for 'self-esteem', which is a refined and a dignified term to be used for oneself. 'He possessed a high self-esteem of him.' 'Worth' means 'value' which is often coupled with terms or sentences like, 'She has no worth of her own. Or she is a worthless person.' A sort of negativity is implicit in the term worth.

sell/sell to/sell off/sell out

Like so many other words, 'sell' also provides several meanings when it is suffixed with prepositions. 'Sell to' is used when one says: 'I shall sell it to you when you like to buy it.' 'Sell off' means 'to sell cheaply'. 'She sold the fruits off (sold cheaply) to go home early today.' 'Sell out' implies 'to indicate putting in a part or all of one's shares in a business'. 'I sold out my all the shares to a new company.'

semiweekly/biweekly

'Biweekly' implies something occurring every two weeks' duration, and 'semiweekly' means twice a week, but to avoid any confusion better say, 'every other week' or 'twice a week'.

send away/send down/send for/send in/send off

Like some other words 'send' provides several meanings when suffixed or prefixed with adjectives or prepositions. For example, 'send away' means 'to dismiss or order from a distance'. 'I sent my servant away for he was not of much use to us.' 'Send down' implies 'dismissal from a school or college on account of misconduct'. 'He was sent down from the college on account of his misconduct.' 'Send for' means 'to ask or to order to come'. 'Don't remove anything from this room unless I send for it.' 'Send in' implies 'send for some competition or exhibition'. 'Send in her name for the music competition to day.' 'Send off' refers to a 'situation when someone is leaving for good and people gather to see him off'. 'We gave a hearty send off to our retiring Manager today.'

sense/since

'Sense' is a verb, which means 'feel' or 'good judgement' or 'intellect'. 'She has a good sense of conceiving matters which apparently don't look clear.' 'Since' is an adverb and can be used in different situations in a sentence. 'Since (point of time) you have gone I have not visited the market.' 'I did not like to discuss further in the meeting, since (because) you were not there.'

sensual/sensuous

These two terms are slightly difficult to understand clearly. 'Sensual' normally refers to physical desires and also experiences involving sex. 'Sensuous' is often referred to aesthetic happiness such as 'sensuous paintings' or 'sensuous music'. 'Sensuous' also means 'sumptuous' or 'luxurious'. 'Your car looks very sensuous from outside.'

separate/seperate

'Separate' means 'divide' or 'split' or 'break up'. 'Don't you ever try to separate these two friends?' 'Separate' is often misspelled as 'seperate'.

set apart/set back/set down/set off/set on/set out

Like some other words 'set' is also a term, that if suffixed or prefixed with an adjective or a preposition provides several meanings. 'Set' means 'to move or place so as to reach it'. 'Set apart' implies 'to put on one side for future use'. 'Please set your personal malice apart and become good friends again.' 'Set back' implies 'to move back'. 'Could you set the hands of the clock back?' 'Set down' implies 'allow to get down or to get out'. 'They stopped the car to let one person set down'. 'Set off' implies 'to start'. 'He will set off for Delhi tomorrow.' 'Set on' means 'to go forward or to attack'. 'A mad dog set on them while they were strolling.' 'Set out' implies 'to begin a journey'. 'She set out for Delhi with good feelings.'

setup/set up

'Setup' implies 'system'. 'Set up' could mean 'to fix or arrange something'. 'The setup you have in mind can be set up well if you have finances for it.'

settle/settle down/settle for/settle on/settle with

'Settle' implies 'to establish'. 'Settle down' means 'to sit or lie comfortably'. It also implies 'establishing at a place'. 'We have settled down in this town for we liked it.' 'Please settle down on this bed'. 'Settle for' means 'to accept but not quite satisfactorily'. 'When I sold my house, I had to settle for a price that was not very suitable for me.' 'Settle on' means 'to decide' or 'to give for use during one's life time'. 'I have decided to settle my property on my eldest son.' 'Settle with' implies to pay what one owes to'. 'He has agreed to settle with the loan on the last day of this month.'

several/various

Both the words could be quite tricky while using them in spoken or written English. When one uses 'several', he has number in his mind. 'I met several people in the theatre.' But if you say: 'I met various people in the theatre, it could mean 'different kinds of (many) people.'

shepherd/Shepard

When 'Shepard' is capitalised, it could mean the family name but 'shepherd' simply means a person who has herds of sheep.

sherbert/sherbet

'Sherbet' means an icy dessert or drink, taken from Persian background. 'Sherbert' is sometimes misused in place of 'sherbet'.

shock/electrocute

'Shock' means 'alarm' or 'upset' or 'distress'. 'I was shocked to hear the news of my friend's accident.' 'The court ordered to electrocute (killing by using electricity) the criminal.'

silicon/silicone

'Silicon' is a chemical element while 'silicones' are plastics that contain 'silicon'.

simile

A 'simile' is a parallel symbol. 'She has a moon-like face.'

simple/simplistic

'Simple' means 'easy' or 'straightforward'. 'He is a simple person.' 'He is a simplistic (too simple) person.'

slash/backslash

'Backslash' is this: \. It leans backwards and is different from a regular lash. Slashes are often used in computer systems to indicate directories or subdirectories. They need to be used carefully.

slight of hand/sleight of hand

The proper word is 'sleight of hand' not slight of hand. Sleight means 'trick or skill' and when we add 'hand' to it, it becomes trick of hand. 'Some people are good at sleight of hand.' 'Her sleight-of-hand skills were phenomenally great.'

sluff off/slough off

'Slough off' implies 'get rid of something like dried skin'. 'Sluff off' is neither a correct term, nor commonly used by people.

snuck/sneaked

Both the terms are past tense of sneak. Snuck is accepted in American English, while sneaked is a traditional word.

societal/social

In fact, both societal and social mean almost one and the same thing except that societal is rarely used for the term social. Societal refers to 'relating to society' while social may have several other connotations too.

sojourn/journey

'Sojourn' implies 'one's temporary stay at one place'. 'Mr. X sojourns at places for sightseeing only.' 'Journey' implies travelling.

sometime/some time

When one word form (sometime) is used, it indicates indefinite time. 'Can you please meet me sometime in my office?' When one says, 'I like to see you some time this week in my office.' It implies some sort of definiteness, as he/she has to find some time to see him during the week.

somewhat of a/somewhat/something of a

The best thing would be to use 'somewhat' only out of the three phrases as it conveys what one wants to convey. 'You look somewhat (rather or a bit) puzzled today.'

sort of/kind of

These two terms are used as slangs while one is indulged in a casual conversation with someone. 'It was a sort of (kind of) an unruly place full of noise and disorder.'

soup of the day

Such an expression (originated from French) is exhibited in restaurants telling what special soup they have prepared that day for the customers. It is just a way of attracting customers.

sour grapes

'Sour grapes' has nothing to do with the sour taste of grapes, but currently it would be more suitable an expression denoting a difficult task, like someone thinking or planning to be rich by visiting Las Vegas and indulging in gambling, and hoping to win a lot of money. It has nothing to do with the old story that conveys how a fox, when unable to reach the grapes, said inadvertently, "The grapes are sour."

stain glass/stained glass

'Stained glass' is the correct term and not stain glass. 'Stained means 'tainted' or 'marked' or 'blemished'. 'I can easily spot out a stained glass on the table.'

stalactite/stalagmite

'Stalagmite' usually refers to a calcium carbonate deposit resembling an inverted 'stalactite', formed on the floor of a cave by the dripping of percolating calcareous water.

stamp/stomp

Both the terms provide the same meaning except that stomp is used colloquially. In a formal conversation, stamp is considered better.

step/step aside/step down/step in/step off/step up

Like so many other words 'step' also provides several meanings when prefixed or suffixed with an adjective or a preposition. 'Step' means move one foot after the other — forward. 'Step aside' implies 'move to one side'. 'Please step aside to accommodate my friend'. 'Step down' means 'to resign or to leave a position'. 'The senior brother stepped down from his position in the company to give chance to his junior brother.' 'Step in' implies 'intervening'. 'You must step in immediately in your family affairs before things go to the point of no return.' 'Step off' (out) means 'measuring by taking steps'. 'Please step out a couple of yards from this point.' 'Step up' implies 'to fix or to increase'. 'Better step up your efforts to complete the assignment on time.'

strike down/strike off/strike on/strike through/ strike up

'Strike' means 'to hit or to give a blow'. When a preposition or an adjective is prefixed or suffixed to 'strike', it also provides different meanings. 'Strike down' implies 'hitting hard to make him/her fall on to the ground'. 'As soon as he spotted him, he struck him down.' 'Strike off' means 'cut off with a blow or to remove'. 'My friend's name was struck off by the teacher on account of his long absence from the class.' 'Strike on' means 'getting in suddenly'. 'A thought struck on my mind all of a sudden.' 'Strike through' implies 'cross out or to put a line'. 'The examiner was irritated to read the answer and instantly struck it through.' 'Strike up' means 'begin to play'. 'He gradually struck up acquaintance with the lady sitting by his side in the bus.'

stationary/stationery

When something is still and standing without moving, it is 'stationary'. A piece of paper or a similar material is just a 'stationery'.

stereo

A 'stereo' refers to a device or a means of producing sound in two or more channels to give an effect of three-dimensional sound. Most people are familiar with this sort of a device.

straightjacket/straitjacket

'Straitjacket' literally means 'a narrow confining piece of clothing' but frequently referring to a 'narrow-minded person'. Some people by mistake use it as straightjacket, as the spellings of both the terms are so close. 'It is often observed that even highly educated persons sometimes behave like straitjacketed persons.'

substance-free

At times some over-enthusiastic persons use certain terms in speech which do not make any sense. One of such expressions is 'substance-free'. What someone may mean by it is 'to be free from the use of illegal drugs and alcohol.' It would be better to say: 'I would like to have a drug and alcohol free environment.'

substitute with/substitute for

The correct use of the phrase is 'substitute for', and not 'substitute with'. 'Peanuts are great substitute for cashew nuts.'

subtle/suttle

'Subtle' means 'slight' or 'faint'. 'There is a subtle difference in these two shirts as far as their design is concerned.' 'Suttle' is often wrongly used for subtle.

suffer with/suffer from

A person does not suffer with but 'suffers from' a disease.

suit/suite

You stay in a hotel at times in a 'suite' but when you go to bed you wear a night 'suit'.

summary/summery

'Summary' means 'digest' or a 'synopsis'. 'Please give me only the summary of the report you have received from the company.' 'Summery' refers to the warm weather only.

supercede/supersede

'Supersede' means 'to sit high' or 'to replace'. 'The new boss superseded the old one two days back.' 'Supercede' is erroneously used in place of supersede.

supine/prone

'Supine' implies 'lying on the back with face upwards'. Prone is just opposite to supine. 'Prone' means 'lying flat with face down'. It would be better to remember at least one correctly so that one does not make any mistakes in their use.

supplement/supplementary

'Supplement' means 'something (a thing) added to something else to improve or complete it'. 'I need to work in the evening after my office is over, to supplement my income.' 'Supplementary' means 'additional or extra'. Someone is offering a gift to a friend and says: 'This is supplementary to the main gift I gave you this morning.'

supposably/supposedly

'Supposedly' is the correct and standard term and not 'supposably', which sometimes is used by mistake.

suppose to/supposed to

The correct term is 'supposed to' and not 'suppose to'. 'You are supposed to remember the right phrase and not the incorrect one.'

supremist/supremacist

'Supremacist' is an advocate of group supremacy. 'Supremacist' is the correct term and often spelt by mistake as 'supremist'.

T

tact/tack

'Tact' is related to the skill in taking abrupt turns while boating. At times one has to take abrupt turns while boating. It all depends on one's being skilful. Therefore it may also mean 'to try different approaches while taking decisions'. 'Tack' implies 'direction' or 'course' or 'approach'. Though both the terms look almost alike, they are quite apart as far as their applications are concerned.

taken back/taken aback

'Taken aback' implies 'startled or amazed by something'. 'I was taken aback by her sudden appearance at the meeting.' 'Taken back' implies 'to go to past'. 'Your story took me back to our college days abruptly.'

taught/taut

'Taut' implies 'rigid' or 'stretched tight'. 'He pulled the rope quite taut.' 'She taught Maths today in the class.'

teenage/teenaged

The traditional term is 'teenaged' but 'teenage' is also accepted now.

tenant/tenet

A 'tenant' is a person who leases an apartment from someone. A 'tenet' is a principle or faith that people hold in their minds. 'I love to follow Buddha's tenets.'

tender hooks/tenterhooks

'Tenterhooks' conveys the sense of 'to be in a tense state of mind with anticipation like a stretched canvas'. Perhaps the phrase is taken or its meaning inferred from 'tenter' which means a canvas-stretcher. 'My brother looks to be on tenterhooks these days as his examination results are expected.' 'Tender hooks' is not a prevalent phrase.

tentative

'Tentative' implies 'unsure' or 'provisional'. 'What I have said just now is a tentative plan. The actual planning will be done only when all the results relating the issue are known.'

than/then

When we are involved with comparing two things, we use 'than'. 'She looks more relaxed these days than before.' 'Then' invariably refers to time. 'When you will reach home, then (at that time) I shall ring him up.'

thankyou/thank you

'Thank you' is a two word phrase and 'thankyou' is not a correct term.

thaw/unthaw

The right term is 'thaw' which means 'melt' or defrost'. 'The continued warm weather has resulted in an unexpected thaw.' 'Unthaw' is not a commonly used term.

therefor/therefore

The most commonly accepted term is 'therefore' not 'therefor'.

these kind/this kind

Since the term 'these' can be used as a plural form, we need to add 's' to kind (kinds) such as, 'these kinds of things,' etc. 'This kind' is a correct term and can be used as: 'This kind of conversation seems to be entertaining.'

these ones/these

'These ones' or 'these' both are correct. It depends how one likes to use them in a context. 'These ones (grapes or oranges or any thing) seem to be good to buy.' 'These are good fruits to buy.'

think on/think about

'Think on' is now less in use and in its place 'think about' is more acceptable. 'Think about the people who don't possess much warm clothes in winter.'

though/thought/through

The difference in the meanings of these terms is very obvious but sometimes people make mistakes in their spellings. It is better to remember one or two of the correct spellings to avoid any mistakes in their use. 'Though her thought and viewpoint was correct, I could not get through as per her advice.'

till/until

Both these words are correct and are in use, except that it depends how one uses them in a sentence. 'I shall be in this office till 6 o'clock.' 'I shall not leave here until you are back from home.'

titled/entitled

'Titled' and 'entitled' both are correct terms. 'Entitled' has been in use since long and not very far back from now, some writers have also been using the term 'titled' like, 'The book is titled *Mahabharata for Children*.'

tolled/told

Perhaps the right expression is 'all told' and not 'tolled'. 'Tolled' could be rooted from 'toll' that means 'tax' or 'fee' or 'levy' taken for the development of roads or bridges, etc. 'Told' is the past tense of 'tell'.

tongue and cheek/tongue in cheek

When sometimes people are in a mood to kidding and deliberately utter a wrong thing, others like to keep their tongues in their cheeks. Therefore, the correct expression at such a situation is 'tongue in cheek' not 'tongue and cheek'.

toward/towards

The term 'towards' is acceptable in the U.K., and 'toward' is used in the U.S. Both the terms are interchangeable and mean the same.

tradegy/tragedy

People mispronounce 'tragedy' as 'tradegy' and also misspell it. The correct term is 'tragedy', which is related to the word 'tragic', meaning 'sad' or disastrous'.

troop/troupe

A group of artistes or performers could be a 'troupe' but a group of military personnel is known as a 'troop'. 'It was a fine troupe of seasoned artistes.'

truely/truly

Several people are mixed up with the correct spelling of 'truly' and write it as 'truely' instead. Perhaps the mistake occurs on account of the root term 'true'.

U

ulterior/alterior

'Ulterior' implies 'hidden' or 'concealed'. 'When she says that she has no desire to see her friend any more, she has some ulterior motive.' 'Alterior' is not a correct term to be used for 'ulterior'. Such mistakes occur on account of mispronouncing the terms.

unconscience/unconscious

There is nothing like 'unconscience'. The correct term is 'unconscious' which means 'lifeless' or 'insensible'. 'When I went to see him in the hospital, he was unconscious.'

unique

Sometimes some people don't exactly know the correct use of the term 'unique' and misconceive it as something strange or misfit or something not proper, taking it in a negative manner. On the contrary, the term means 'only one of its kind' or 'exclusive' or 'exceptional' or 'inimitable'. 'The landscape that the artist painted was just unique.' It would mean that the painting was unparalleled.

unloosen/loosen

'Unloosen' would mean 'tighten or not loosening'. 'Loosen' implies to 'undo' or to 'release'. 'Please loosen the horses right now.'

unrest

At times media may use the term 'unrest' to denote some social disorder but if there are riots in which people are killed or bullets are fired, unrest is a very mild term to indicate the situation.

upmost/utmost

'Utmost' is the correct term, not 'upmost'. 'My utmost (greatest or chief) intention to keep him on the committee is to ensure his cooperation and help.'

use to/used to

It is 'used to' that we 'use to' denote some habitual action or perpetual habit, not 'use to'. 'I used to visit her regularly when I was a student in the college twenty years back.'

V

vague

'Vague' implies 'unclear' or 'indistinct'. 'Her comments about her sister were so vague that we could not infer anything from them about her.' Very often people go on talking (or writing) about things which are not directly related to the main topic. 'This kind of talk or writing could be taken as vague.'

vain/vane/vein

There is a subtle difference between these three terms. One needs to know it very carefully. 'If a person is possessed with vanity (pride and egotism), he/she is a vain person.' 'Vain' also implies 'fruitless'. 'All her care and love for her children went in vain.' 'A vane is a movable device fixed to a high object to show wind direction.' 'Vein means tubular branching vessels that carry blood towards heart.'

vale of tears/ veil of tears

'Vale (valley) of tears' is the appropriate phrase indicating that life is 'full of sorrow and difficulties'. 'Veil of tears' is an incorrect expression.

valuble/valuable

'Valuable' is a correct term, which at times is mispronounced and misspelled too, as 'valuble'.

various/several

'Various implies 'different' not exactly 'several'. Better use 'several' when you mean to indicate a good number. 'I met in the meeting several people who possessed similar opinion on the issue.'

vary/differ

Our views may 'differ' because we may 'vary' (diverge) on several issues. In fact, there is no subtle difference in these two terms. It depends on how one makes a correct use of them in a context.

verbage/verbiage

'Verbiage' implies 'a lot of useless words in writing or speech.' 'There was a lot of verbiage in the politician's speech, but little information.'

verses/versus

'Verses' are the lines of poetry.' 'Versus' means 'against' or 'in opposition to'. 'North Delhi football team will play a match versus South Delhi team.'

very/so

Both 'very' and 'so' convey the same sense except that 'very' is used more in speech while 'so' in writing. 'I am so pleased to receive your letter.' 'Oh! I am very delighted to see you.'

very/vary

'Vary' implies 'change' or means 'diverge'. 'These two patterns on this piece of cloth vary too much.' 'I am very happy to meet you this morning.'

very/much

There is a slight difference in the meaning and application of these two terms. 'I frequently met her in very different places.' 'Many times she possessed moods that were much different from her previous moods.'

vice versa/visa versa

'Vice versa' which means 'just opposite' is the correct term and not 'visa versa'. 'On one Sunday I went to see her. On the next Sunday she visited me. Then we met each other vice versa.'

vicious circle/vicious cycle

'Vicious circle' is the correct phrase in use except that some people may use it as a 'vicious cycle' just to jeer at others.

villian/villain

'Villain' is the correct word meaning 'rogue' or scoundrel', not 'villian'. 'My neighbour is a villain and cannot be trusted in any serious enterprises.'

vinegarette/vinaigrette

'Vinaigrette' is a classic French dressing (applied on eatables and salads) and often misspelled as 'vinegrette'.

viola/voila

A musical instrument or a flower is known as a 'viola'. 'Voila' has originated from French, implying 'beholding'.

visable/visible

'Visible' means 'clearly seen or visible'. 'Visable' is not the correct spelling for visible. 'Everything is clearly visible from this point.'

vitae/vita

Both 'vitae' and 'vita' refer to 'one's brief autobiographical description'. Vita has been driven from *vitae.* 'Please send your complete curriculum vitae with the application.'

vocal chords/vocal cords

The cords attached to our vocal parts are at times misspelled as 'chords' which are commonly used with terms like music or musical chords.

vocation/avocation

'Avocation is related to one's hobbies. 'Vocation' is related to one's job. 'What avocations do you pursue during your long vacations?'

volumptuous/voluptuous

'Voluptuous' implies 'lumpiness' and 'luxurious'. 'She possesses a very voluptuous figure.' 'Volumptuous' is an incorrect spelling.

vunerable/vulnerable

'Vulnerable' means 'susceptible' or 'weak'. 'Our doors are vulnerable to theft as they are very fragile.'

W

wait/wait for/wait up/wait upon

'Wait' means 'to stay where one is 'or 'delay acting until it (one) comes'. 'Wait for' is also used in similar situations. 'Please wait for me until I am back.' 'Wait up' implies 'to stay up and not to go to bed' 'Could you please wait up until I am back from work?' 'Wait upon' means 'to act as a servant' or 'as a helper'. 'Some men like to wait upon their women (wives).'

walk/walk about/walk away from/ walk away with/ walk out/walk over

Like so many words in English, 'walk' carries several meanings when prefixed or suffixed with a preposition or an adjective. 'Walk about' implies 'journey' or 'meeting people informally'. 'I like to walk about occasionally.' 'When the Senator comes to this town, he likes to walk about to acquaint himself with the people.' 'Walk away from' implies 'beating easily in a contest'. 'Sheela walked away from all her classmates in a hundred metre race today.' 'Walk away with' means 'to win easily' or 'carry off' or 'to take'. 'Padukone walked away with the badminton trophy in England several years ago.' 'Walk out' means 'to go on strike'. 'The factory workers walked out in protest against the poor wages.' 'Walk over' implies 'accede defeat easily'. 'My opponent gave me a walk over in tennis semi-finals.'

wipe/wipe away/wipe off/wipe out/wipe up

'Wipe' means to 'clean or dry by rubbing with a cloth' or 'paper'. 'Please wipe this table properly.' 'Wipe away' (wipe off) means 'to remove by wiping'. 'Try hard to wipe away the stain on this shirt.' 'Wipe out' means to 'get rid of' or 'remove'. 'Please wipe out your old enmity with Shyam.' 'Wipe up' means 'to take up (liquid)'. 'Will you please wipe up the spilt milk from the floor?'

warrantee/warranty

'Warrantee' is 'a person against whom a warrant (legal notice) is issued'. People often get confused and use it for 'warranty' which means a sort of 'guarantee' or 'contract' or a 'pledge'. 'We warranty that the article will last at least one year after you start using it.'

wary/weary

'Wary' means 'cautious' or 'suspicious'. People at times use 'wary' for 'weary' which means 'tired' or sleepy'. 'I am quite weary today.'

way more/far more/much more

In fact, 'way more' is not the usual term to use it for 'far more'. 'If you go a little far more than two miles you can spot out the place you are looking for.' However, some people may say, 'She is now much more popular than before', to express the intensity of popularity. Even if you use 'much popular' it will serve the purpose.

ways/way

In standard English, the correct use is 'way' and not 'ways' which sometimes people use in speech. 'If you adopt a right way, you will hardly fail in your mission.'

weather/wether/whether

'Weather' is related to the climate. 'We like to hear everyday weather report on television.' 'Whether' indicates some sort of 'uncertainty'. 'Whether she should stay or go, I am yet not certain about it.' 'Wether' is a 'castrated male sheep'.

whereabouts are/whereabouts is

In spite of the fact that the term 'whereabouts' looks plural, its use in English is as a singular word. 'His whereabouts is not known to me often.'

while away/wile away

'While away' is the standard and traditional phrase which is used to convey 'waste' or 'destroy' or 'idle away'. 'Please don't while away your time or it will waste you away.' 'Wile away' is neither correct nor much in use.

whilst/while

Both 'whilst' and 'while' are acceptable. 'Whilst' is an Americanised term and 'while' is an old English term.

whisky/whiskey

'Whisky' is a British term, while 'whiskey' is an American one. Both the terms convey the same meaning.

who/whom

There is a great confusion in the use of these two words which often convey the same sense, although most people like to use 'who' in place of 'whom' these days. To avoid any confusion, it is better to use 'who' as a subject of a question sentence and 'whom' as an object in a sentence. 'Who is coming for the dinner tonight?' 'I shall give this book to him whom I think to be the best in the class.' Examine this example to appreciate the use of the term 'who' in place of 'whom': 'Who are you looking for?'

wholely/wholly

'Wholly' is the correct term not 'wholely'.

who's/whose

When we use a word like 'who's' it indicates 'who is' or 'who has' and not 'whose'. Possessive pronouns don't ever take apostrophes. 'Who's coming for the dinner' would mean 'who is coming for the dinner'.

will/shall

Gradually 'will' has replaced 'shall', especially in American English. Traditionally the terms are used as: 'I shall come if you so wish. I (we) will come if you so wish.' Use of 'will' with I and we indicates some sort of surety.

wimp/whimp

Most common use of the term is 'wimp' which implies 'a weakling' or a coward'. 'Oh! He is much of a wimp.' 'Whimp' is not a correct word. It is also not in a common use for 'wimp'.

without further adieu/without further ado

'Ado' means 'without any delay or fuss'. It has perhaps become popular after one of Shakespeare's plays, *Much Ado About Nothing*. The right phrase is 'without further ado'.

world-renown/world-renowned

The correct term is 'world-renowned'. 'Pt. J.L. Nehru is a world-renowned personality.'

worst comes to worse/worst comes to worst

The age-old use of the correct term is 'worst comes to worst' and not 'worst comes to worse'. It simply means that even if 'bad things happen or difficulties come or even if any losses are incurred', etc. 'Worst comes to worst that I may sustain great losses, I will always stand by you.'

would have liked/would have liked to have

'Would have liked to have' implies 'the implicit desire to have it or to do it'. Some people may use 'would have liked' in its place by mistake or because of lack of adequate understanding of the correct meaning of the term. 'I would have liked to have another cup of milk if you had offered it to me right then.' It conveys, 'I had a desire to have an additional cup of milk, but you did not offer it to me'.

wreckless/reckless

'Reckless' means 'thoughtless' or 'irresponsible'. 'My brother is not as reckless as your younger brother is.' 'Wreckless' is not a correct term to be used for reckless.

writting/writing

'Writing' is the correct spelling of the term, not writting.

wrongly/wrong

One has to be clear while using these two terms. 'She was wrong when she said that her mother would not approve of her meeting me.' 'Her thinking was wrongly influenced by her brother.' 'Wrongly' often precedes the verb it modifies.

X

XL

It is a common abbreviation for 'extra large' or 'extra long'.

XO

'XO' indicates 'executive officer'.

Xmas/Christmas

People often mix up the correct term 'Christmas' with an uncommon abbreviation Xmas, which is also not much in use.

Y

yacht

'Yacht' is usually referred to a large recreational watercraft people love to go on for water sports. The word 'yacht' is also used as a verb, meaning 'to race or cruise in a yacht'.

ya'll/y'all

'Y'all' is normally used when you address two or more people. 'Y'all' is a plural form and it refers to 'you all' during a casual or informal speech when there are more than two persons whom you are addressing. 'Ya'll' is neither correct, nor it is in use commonly.

yet/as of yet

Some people use 'as of yet' in place of 'yet' or 'as yet'. It is better to use simply 'yet' to avoid any confusion.

yoke/yolk

Something that holds two oxen together is known as a 'yoke'. The yellow part of an egg in the centre is its 'yolk'. 'Some people are fond of eating only yolk and not the complete egg.'

your/you're

You cannot improve 'your' health unless 'you're' (you are) sure that you have changed your eating habits.

Words & Phrases that carry Uncommon Meanings

—Dr. A.P. Sharma

he book aims to display uncommon expressions that look common but are uncommon in usage and meaning. The uncommon expressions are interwoven within the conversations fitted into suitable situations. Dialogues containing common and uncommon expressions, phrases and idioms are developed in a most fascinating style displaying a rich vocabulary and appropriate language that provides a modern touch. In this respect, the reader will have a face to face chance to experience varied and trying situations during different sets of conversations.

The book not only provides new vistas of vision as regards learning how to converse with the people, but also extends before the reader new sets of situations, knitted in dialogues, enabling one to enrich his/her linguistic capabilities.

Sentence Correction
for admission to Foreign Universities

—Dr. A.P. Sharma

- ✓ This booklet is intended to teach how to reduce the errors that occur in the Sentence Correction Test for Admission to Foreign Universities.
- ✓ It also teaches us how to locate the various types of errors in sentences.
- ✓ The basic rules of Grammar have been explained briefly and systematically.
- ✓ The examples and exercises given in this booklet will make you familiar with the different types of questions and provide you with sufficient practice to use the different techniques for answering each type of question.
- ✓ There is also a practice test to evaluate your progress and make you perfect.

Perfect Your English

—Manjusha Nambiar

nglish, as we all know, is full of problems for a foreign learner. One of the easiest ways of improving your English is to eliminate the common mistakes from your writing. While some of these problem-points are easy to explain, others cause difficulty even for the advanced students and teachers. For example, how exactly is the present perfect tense used? Is there any difference between far and a long way?

This book is a guide to the questions of this kind. It addresses over 260 points, which regularly cause problems for the foreign learners. The rules and guidelines are given using as little linguistic terminology as possible.

This book is aimed at the students who wish to improve the quality of their sentences. It is compiled for the use at school or at home.

The entries are arranged alphabetically. Each entry contains an explanation of a problem, examples of correct usage and typical mistakes. The explanations are, as far as possible, given in a simple everyday language.

Dictionary of Modern Phrases with Meanings & Usage

—Joel Lyall

he beauty of any language lies in the appropriate usage of a word or phrase. English, too, has its norms and nuances, and one should know the exact meaning and implication of each word. Many words and phrases have intriguing meanings that may not be apparent at first glance.

This is a unique book of its kind, making its appearance in India for the first time. It is a diligent compilation of modern phrases currently in use the world over. The illustrative examples make understanding easy.

This book of modern phrases will help you hone up your grasp and command over the language and pack a punch in your speech and writing. A must for all those who wish to improve their English and communication skill.
